100 ANY-SIZE STAR BLOCKS

by Linda Causee

Whether you are an experienced quilter, making quilts for years, or just a beginner, one of the most difficult parts of the project often is finding the necessary templates if you are a traditional quilter or the paper patterns if you prefer paper piecing.

This book and its enclosed CD can solve that problem. Just place the CD into your computer, click on the block of your choice, in the size that you desire and print out all of the templates or paper patterns you will need for your quilt. If your original templates become worn, or if you need additional pieces, just repeat the process.

If you've forgotten—or if you've never learned—how to make a quilt by either the traditional method or by using the foundation method, we've included some basic directions on page 64. So make a full-size bed quilt, a wall hanging or a miniature quilt. All of the necessary templates or paper pieces are just a click away.

You'll be a quilting star!

LEISURE ARTS, INC
Little Rock, Arkansas

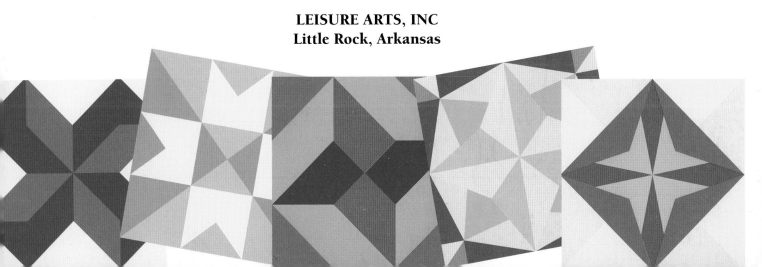

Produced by

Production Team

Creative Directors: Jean Leinhauser
and Rita Weiss
Photography: Carol Wilson Mansfield
Book Design: Linda Causee
Technical Editor: Ann Harnden
Pattern Testers: Annabell Acuavera, Joy
Davis, Candy Flory-Barnes, Faith Horsky,
Ada LeClaire, Pat Ludwick, Wanda
MacLachlan
Machine Quilter: Faith Horsky

Special Thanks to:
Northcott Silks, Inc. for providing the fabrics for:
Rolling Stars Mini quilt, Double Eight-Pointed Stars
Mini Quilt, Tippecanoe Mini Quilt, Royal Diamonds
Mini Quilt and Patriotic Stars Mini Quilt.

Westminister Fibers for providing the fabrics for: Rolling Stars Bed Quilt and Wall Hanging, Double Eight-
Pointed Stars Bed Quilt, Royal Diamonds Wall Hanging
and the Patriotic Stars Bed Quilt.

Fairfield Processing Company for providing batting.

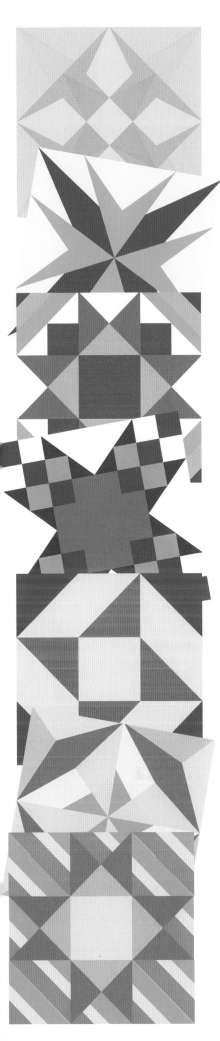

Contents

Before You Start

Choose the block you want to make. Inside this book, you will find a self-loading CD that contains the 100 Star quilt block patterns in seven different sizes. The files on the CD are easily opened using Adobe® Reader®. If you don't have Adobe Reader on your computer, you can get a free download at http://www.adobe.com/. The site provides easy, step-by-step instructions for the download.

When you are ready to make your quilt, simply print out the required number of block patterns for the foundation blocks in Chapters 1, 4 and 5. For the patchwork blocks in chapters 2 and 3, print the patterns in the size you need, then trace the individual pattern pieces onto template plastic. For hand sewing, trace the number of templates needed for your quilt on the wrong side of the fabric. For machine sewing, add $1/4$" seam allowance to each side of the pattern, then cut out your templates.

The blocks on the CD are given as 2", 3", 4", 5", 6", 7", and 8". If you would like your blocks to be larger, use the following guidelines:

9" - use 3" block, enlarge 300%
10" - use 5" block, enlarge 200%
11" - use 3" block, enlarge 367%
12" - use 6" block, enlarge 200%
13" - use 4" block, enlarge 325%
14" - use 7" block, enlarge 200%
15" - use 5" block, enlarge 300%
16" - use 8" block, enlarge 200%

Spinning Star & Whirligig Blocks

Rolling Stars Bed Quilt

Rolling Stars Wall Hanging

Rolling Stars Bed Quilt

Size: 89" x 104"   Block #: 6 Rolling Star
Block Size: 15" x 15" finished   Number of Blocks: 20

MATERIALS

2 yards rosebud print
2 yards light pink
2 yards dark pink (includes second border)
1 1/2 yards light blue
2 yards dark blue (includes first border)
3 yards floral print (includes third border and binding)
7 1/2 yards backing
batting

CUTTING

8 strips, 3"-wide, dark blue (first border)
8 strips, 5"-wide, dark pink (second border)
10 strips, 8"-wide, floral print (third border)
11 strips, 2 1/2"-wide, floral print (binding)

Rolling Stars Wall Hanging

Size: 36 1/2" x 36 1/2"   Block #: 6 Rolling Star
Block Size: 8" x 8" finished   Number of Blocks: 9

MATERIALS

1/2 yard cream (includes second border)
1/2 yard light aqua (includes first border)
1/2 yard medium aqua
1/2 yard medium dark aqua
1 yard dark aqua (includes fourth border and binding)
1/2 yard light coral (includes third border)
1/2 yard dark coral
1 1/8 yards backing
batting

CUTTING

4 strips, 2 1/2"-wide, light aqua (first border)
4 strips, 1 1/2"-wide, cream (second border)
4 strips, 1 1/4"-wide, light coral (third border)
4 strips, 3"-wide, dark aqua (fourth border)
4 strips, 2 1/2"-wide, dark aqua (binding)

Rolling Stars Mini Quilt

Size: 13" x 13"   Block #: 6 Rolling Star
Block Size: 3" x 3" finished   Number of Blocks: 4

MATERIALS

fat quarter white (includes first border)
fat quarter light orange (includes second border and
        binding)
fat quarter dark orange
fat quarter aqua (includes third border)
fat quarter backing
batting

CUTTING

2 strips, 1 1/2"-wide, white (first border)
2 strips, 1"-wide, light orange (second border)
2 strips, 2 1/2"-wide, aqua (third border)
4 strips, 2 1/2"-wide, light orange (binding)

Rolling Stars Mini Quilt

1 Turning Triangles

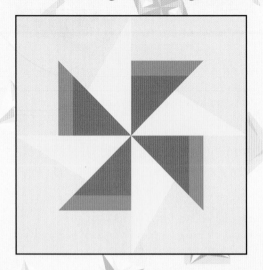

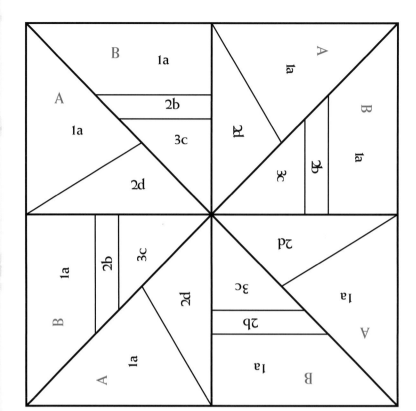

2 Bright Star

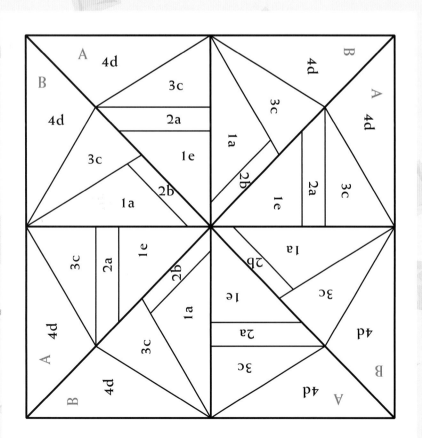

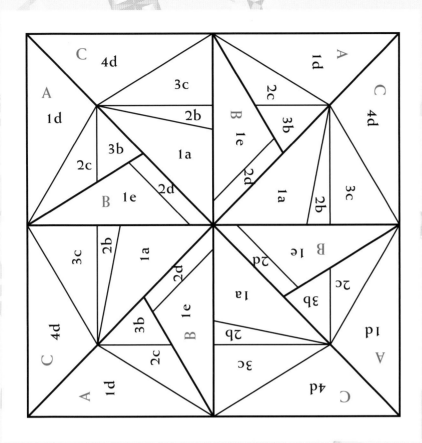

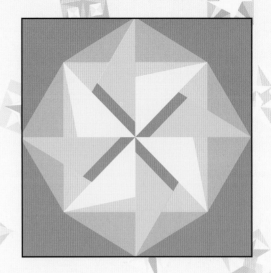

4 Lucky Star

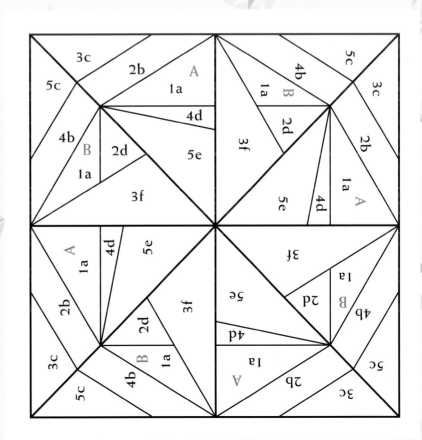

5 Friendship Circle

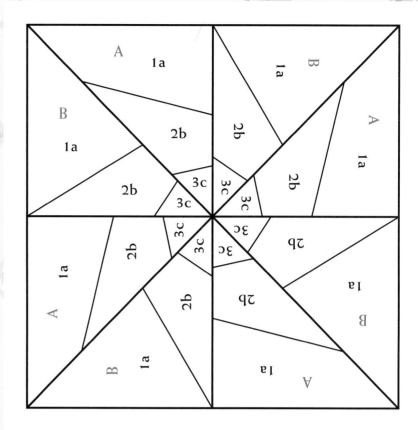

6 Rolling Star

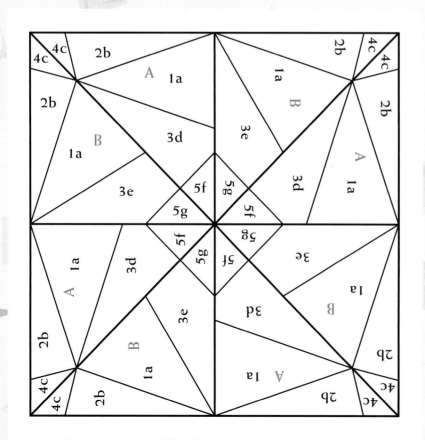

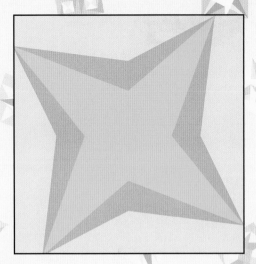

7 Blazing Star

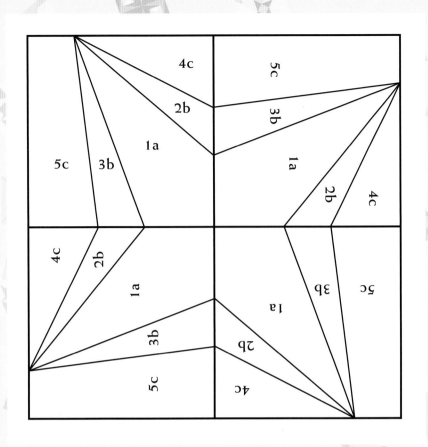

4c	5c
2b	3b
1a	1a
5c 3b	2b
	4c
4c 2b	5c
1a	3b
3b	1a
5c	2b
	4c

8 Windmill

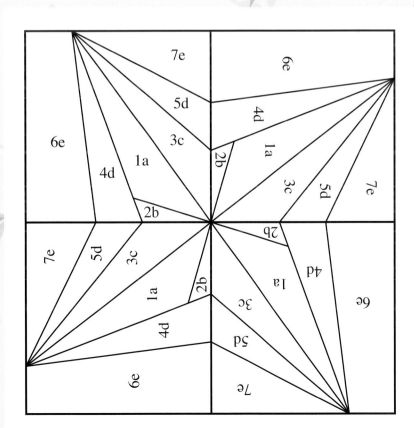

7e	6e
5d	4d
3c	1a
6e	2b
4d	3c
1a	5d
2b	7e
7e	2b
5d	1a
3c	4d
1a	3c
4d	5d
2b	7e
6e	6e

9 Poinsettia

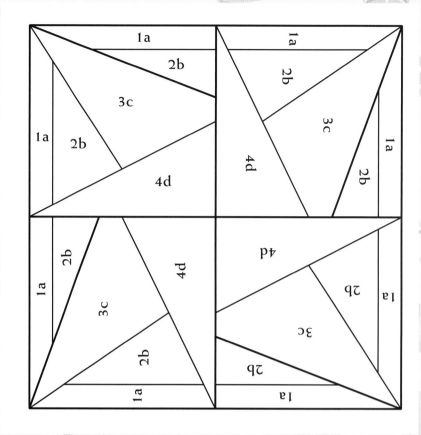

10 Diamond Star

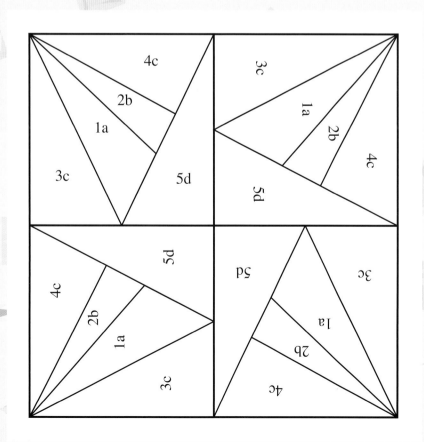

11 Double Star

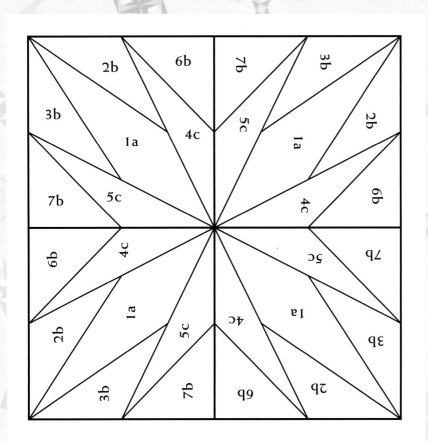

12 Windy Star

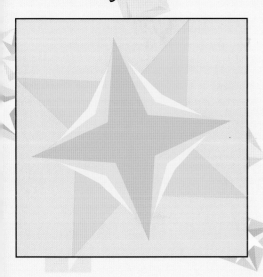

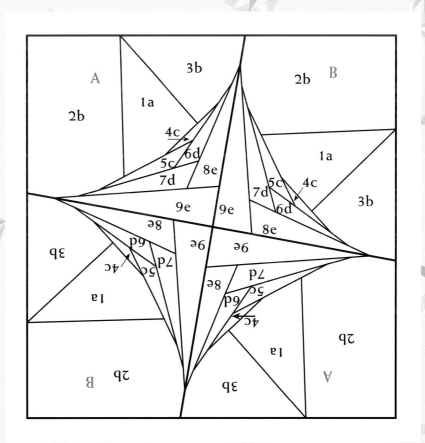

13 Whirligig

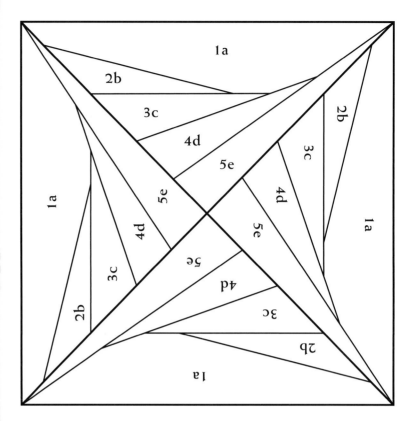

14 Star and Squares

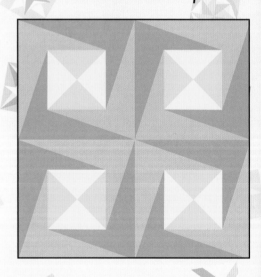

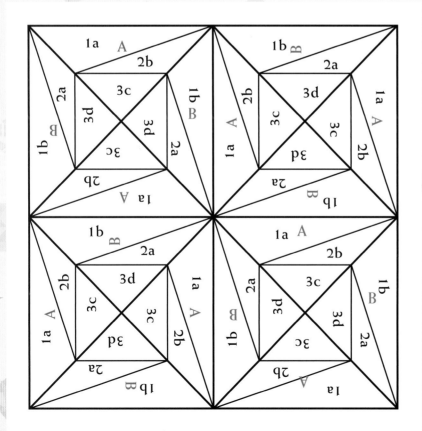

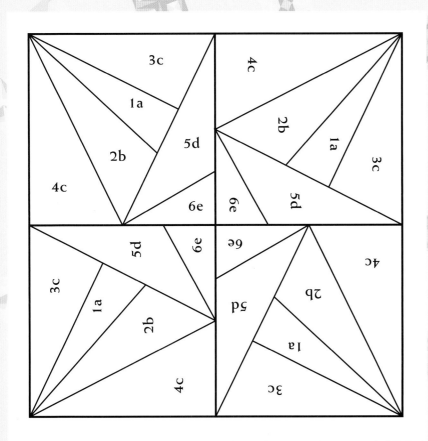

16 *Star in a Roll*

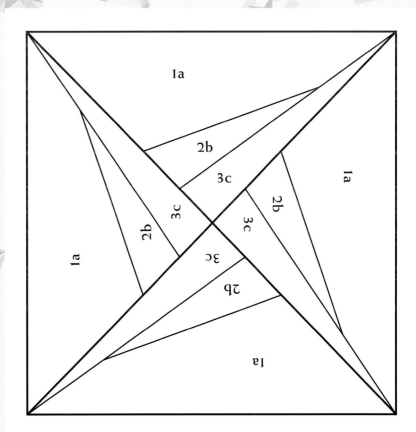

17 Eight-Pointed Star

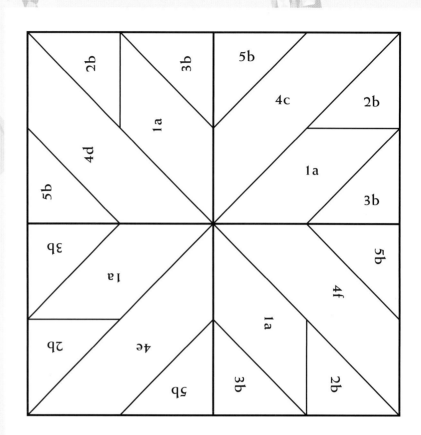

18 Kaleidoscope Star

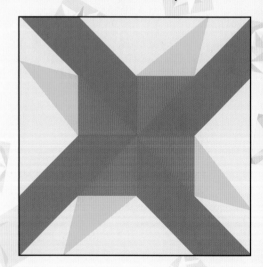

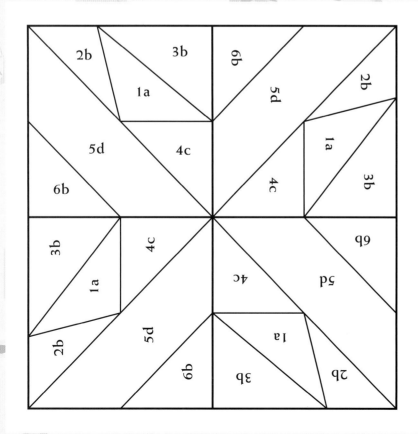

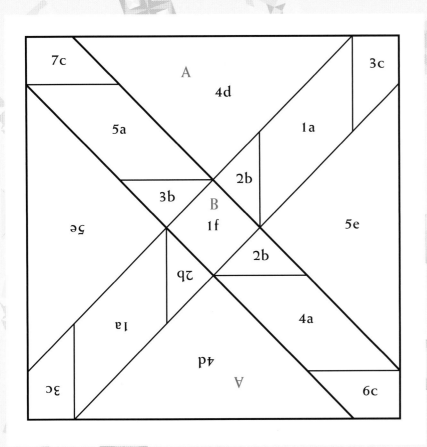

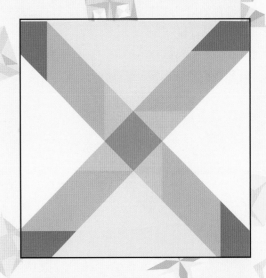

20 *Star and Cross*

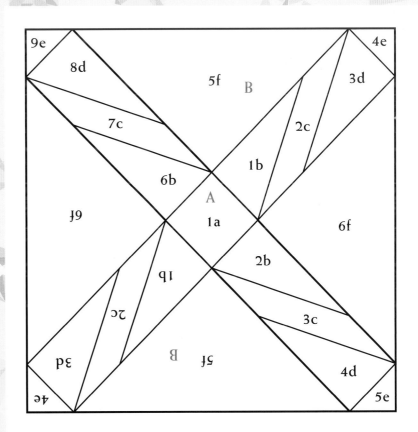

Double Eight-Pointed Star Bed Quilt

Double Eight-Pointed Star Bed Quilt

Size: 68" x 104"
Block Size: 12" x 12" finished

Block #: 28 Double
Eight-Pointed Star
Number of Blocks: 28

MATERIALS
2 yards black print (includes first border)
2 yards aqua print (includes second border)
2 yards lavender/aqua print
2 yards large black/pink print (third border and binding)
6 yards backing
batting

CUTTING
8 strips, 2½"-wide, black print (first border)
8 strips, 4½"-wide, aqua print (second border)
9 strips, 4½"-wide, large black/pink print (third border)
10 strips, 2½"-wide, large black/pink print (binding)

Double Eight-Pointed Star Wall Hanging

Size: 36" x 36"
Block Size: 8" x 8" finished

Block #: 27 Double
Eight-Pointed Star
Number of Blocks: 9

MATERIALS
1 yard gold (includes first border)
1 yard green (includes third border and binding)
1 yard red (includes second border)
1⅛ yards backing
batting

CUTTING
4 strips, 1½"-wide, gold (first border)
4 strips, 2½"-wide, red (second border)
4 strips, 3½"-wide, green (third border)
4 strips, 2½"-wide, green (binding)

Double Eight-Pointed Star Wall Hanging

Double Eight-Pointed Star Mini Quilt

Size: 14" x 14"
Block Size: 4" x 4" finished

Block #: 27 Double
Eight-Pointed Star
Number of Blocks: 4

MATERIALS
fat quarter cream (includes second border and binding)
fat quarter aqua
fat quarter purple (includes first border)
fat quarter backing
batting

CUTTING
4 strips, 1½"-wide, purple (first border)
4 strips, 2½"-wide, cream (second border)
4 strips, 2½"-wide, cream (binding)

Double Eight-Pointed Star Mini Quilt

21 Ohio Star

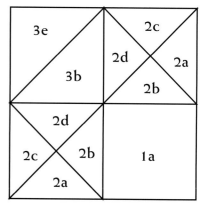

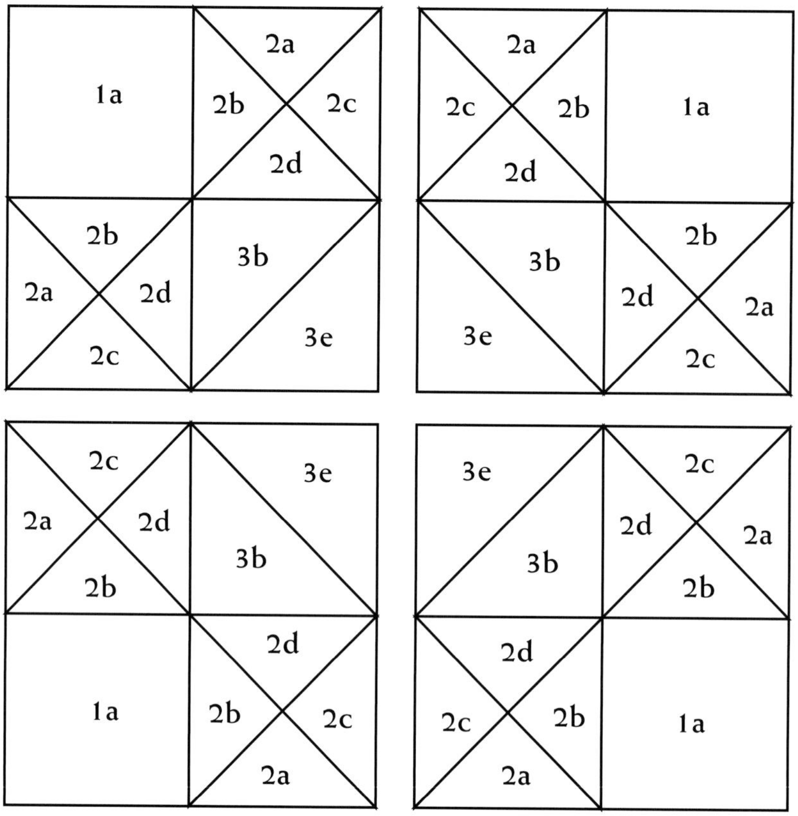

Top-left block:

| 1a | 2a / 2b / 2c / 2d |
| 2b / 2a / 2d / 2c | 3b / 3e |

Top-right block:

| 2a / 2c / 2b / 2d | 1a |
| 3b / 3e | 2b / 2d / 2a / 2c |

Bottom-left block:

| 2c / 2a / 2d / 2b | 3e / 3b |
| 1a | 2d / 2b / 2c / 2a |

Bottom-right block:

| 3e / 2c / 2d / 2a / 2b | 3b |
| 2d / 2c / 2b / 2a | 1a |

22 Beacon

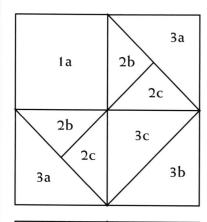

Top-left block:

| 1a | 3a / 2b / 2c |
| 2b / 2c / 3a | 3c / 3b |

Top-right block:

| 3a / 2b / 2c | 1a |
| 3b / 3c | 2b / 2c / 3a |

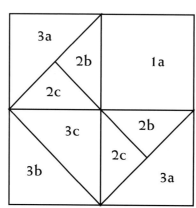

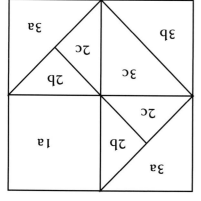

Bottom-left block:

| 3a / 2b / 2c / 3b | 3b / 3c |
| 1a / 2b / 2c | 3a |

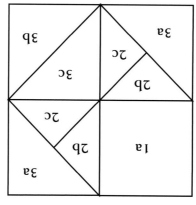

Bottom-right block:

| 3b / 2b / 2c / 3a | 3a / 3c |
| 2c / 2b / 3a | 1a |

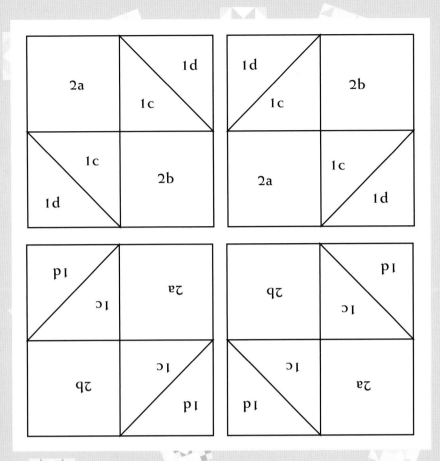

2a	1d
	1c
1c	2b
1d	

1d	2b
1c	
2a	1c
	1d

1d	2a
1c	
2b	1c
	1d

2b	1d
	1c
1c	2a
1d	

24 *Square in a Star*

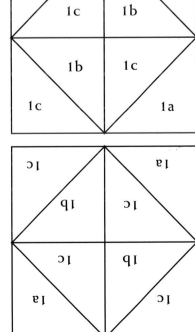

1a		1c
	1c	1b
	1b	1c
1c		1a

1c		1a
	1b	1c
	1c	1b
1a		1c

1c		1a
	1b	1c
	1c	1b
1a		1c

1a		1c
	1c	1b
	1b	1c
1c		1a

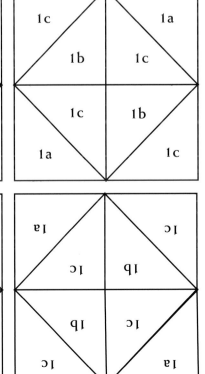

25 Friendship Star

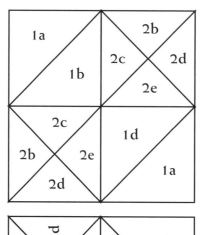

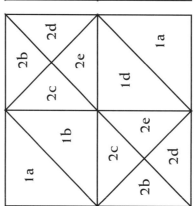

26 Windmill Star

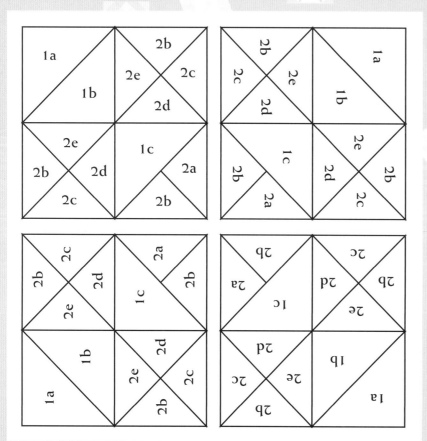

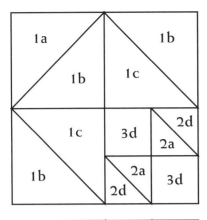
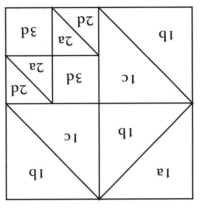

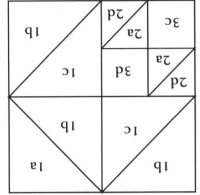
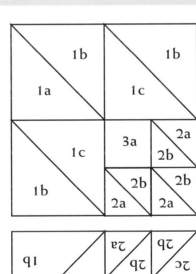

28 Star in a Star

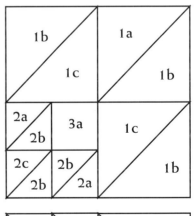
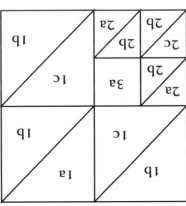
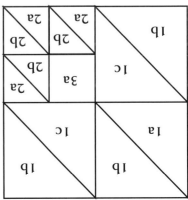

29 New Star

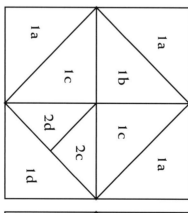

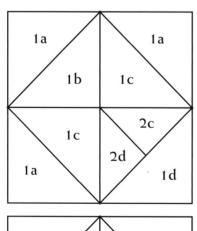

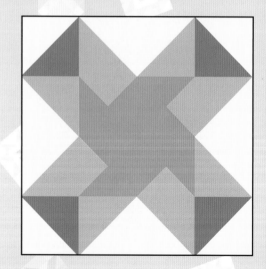

30 Right and Left Star

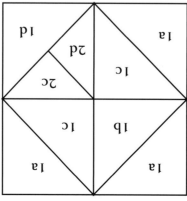

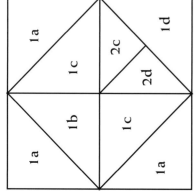

Block 1 (top-left):

1a	2a
	2b
2c	2b
2a	2c

2a	1a
2c	
2c	2b
2b	2a

2a	2b
2b	2c
1a	2c
	2a

2c	2a
2b	2c
2b	1a
2a	

32 Dervish Star

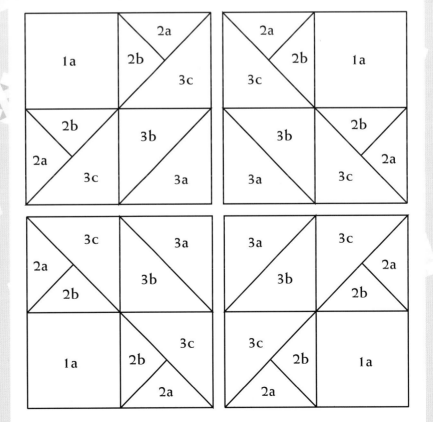

1a	2a
	2b
	3c
2b	3b
2a	
3c	3a

2a	1a
2b	
3c	2b
3b	2a
3a	3c

3c	3a
2a	3b
2b	
1a	3c
2b	
2a	

3a	3c
	2a
3b	2b
3c	
2b	1a
2a	

33 Sarah's Choice

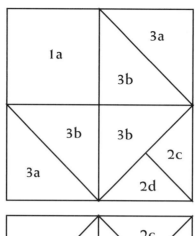

1a	3a
	3b
3b	3b
3a	2c
	2d

3a	1a
3b	
2d	3b	3b
2c	3a

3a	2c
3b	2d
3b	3b
1a	3b
	3a

2d	3a
2c	3b	3b
3b	
3a	1a

34 Martha Washington Star

1b	1a
1a	1c
1c	1c
1a	2b
	2a

1a	1a
	1b
1c	
2a	1c	1c
2b	1a

1a	2b
1c	2a
1c	1c
1b	1c
1a	1a

2a	1a
2b	
1c	1c
1c	1a
1a	1b

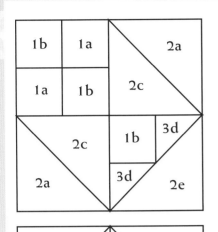

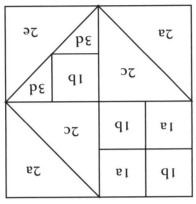

Top-left block:
1b	1a	2a
1a	1b	2c
2c	1b	3d
2a	3d	2e

Top-right block:
2a	1a	1b
2c	1b	1a
3d	1b	2c
2e	3d	2a

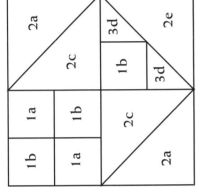

Bottom-left block:
2a	3d	2e
2c	1b	3d
1a	1b	2c
1b	1a	2a

Bottom-right block:
2e	3d	2a
3d	1b	2c
2c	1b	1a
2a	1a	1b

36 Star and Pinwheel

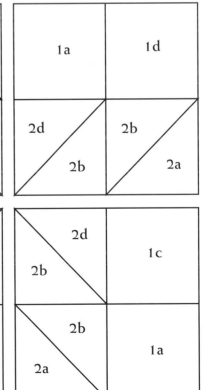

Block 1:
| 1a | 2a / 2b |
| 1c | 2b / 2d |

Block 2:
| 1a | 1d |
| 2d / 2b | 2b / 2a |

Block 3:
| 2a / 2b | 2b / 2d |
| 1d | 1a |

Block 4:
| 2d / 2b | 1c |
| 2b / 2a | 1a |

37 Barbara Frietchie Star

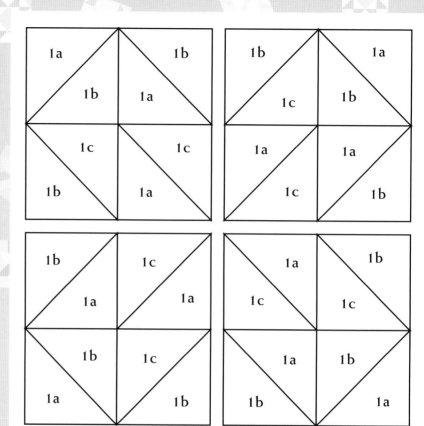

1a	1b
1b	1a
1c	1c
1b	1a

1b	1a
1c	1b
1a	1a
1c	1b

1b	1c
1a	1a
1b	1c
1a	1b

1a	1b
1c	1c
1a	1b
1b	1a

38 Pinwheel Star

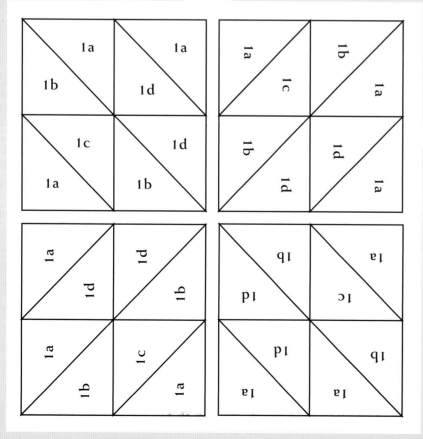

1a	1a
1b	1d
1c	1d
1a	1b

1a	1b
1c	1a
1b	1d
1d	1a

1a	1d
1d	1b
1a	1c
1b	1a

1b	1a
1d	1c
1d	1b
1a	1a

39 *Hither and Yon*

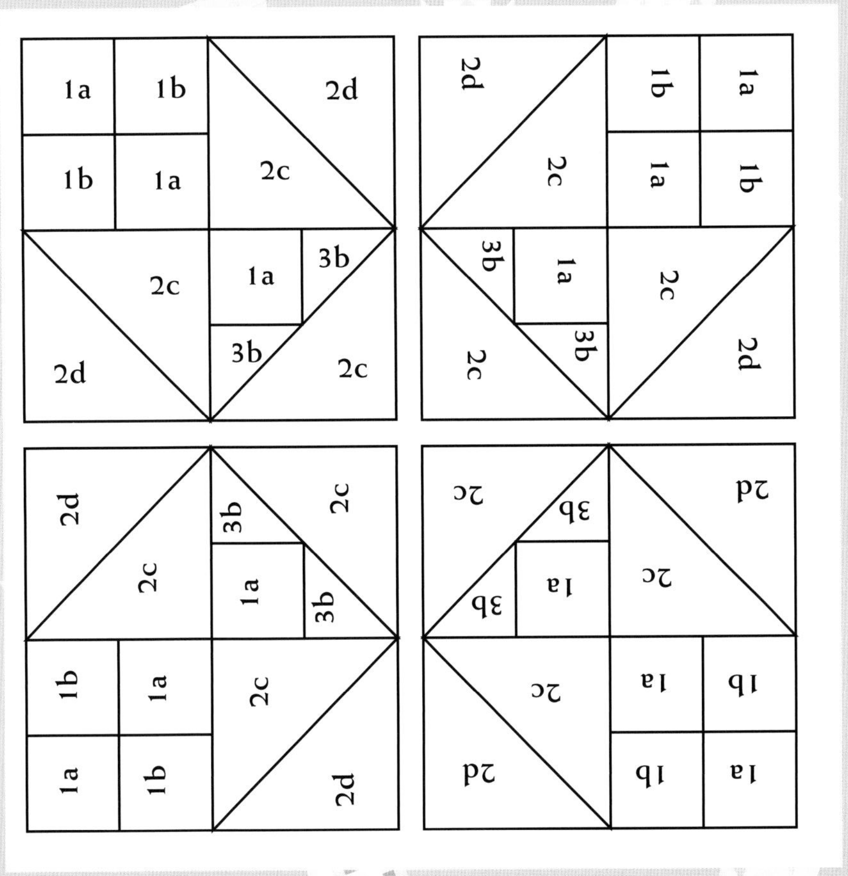
1a 1b 2d
1b 1a 2c
2c 1a 3b
2d 3b 2c
2d 1b 1a
2c 1a 1b
3b 1a 2c
2c 3b 2d
2d 3b 2c
2c 1a 3b
1b 1a 2c
1a 1b 2d
2c 3b 2d
3b 1a 2c
2c 1a 1b
2d 1b 1a

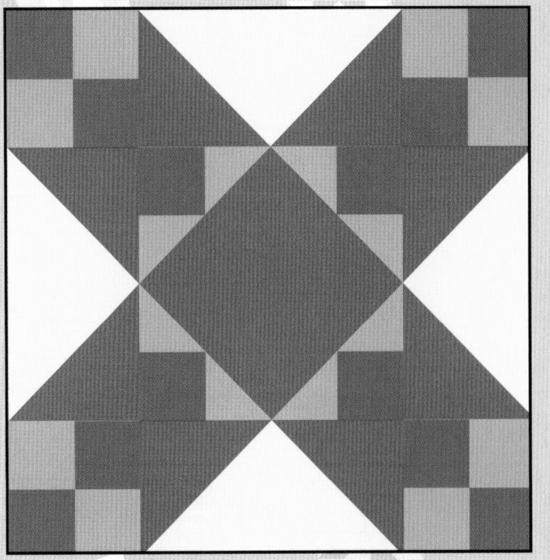

40 *Raz-Ma-Taz*

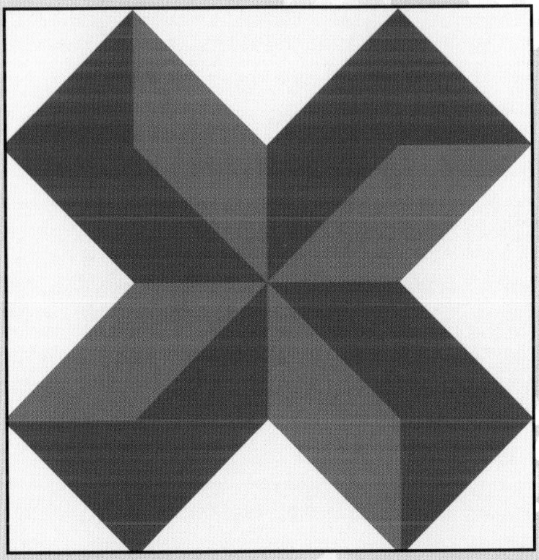

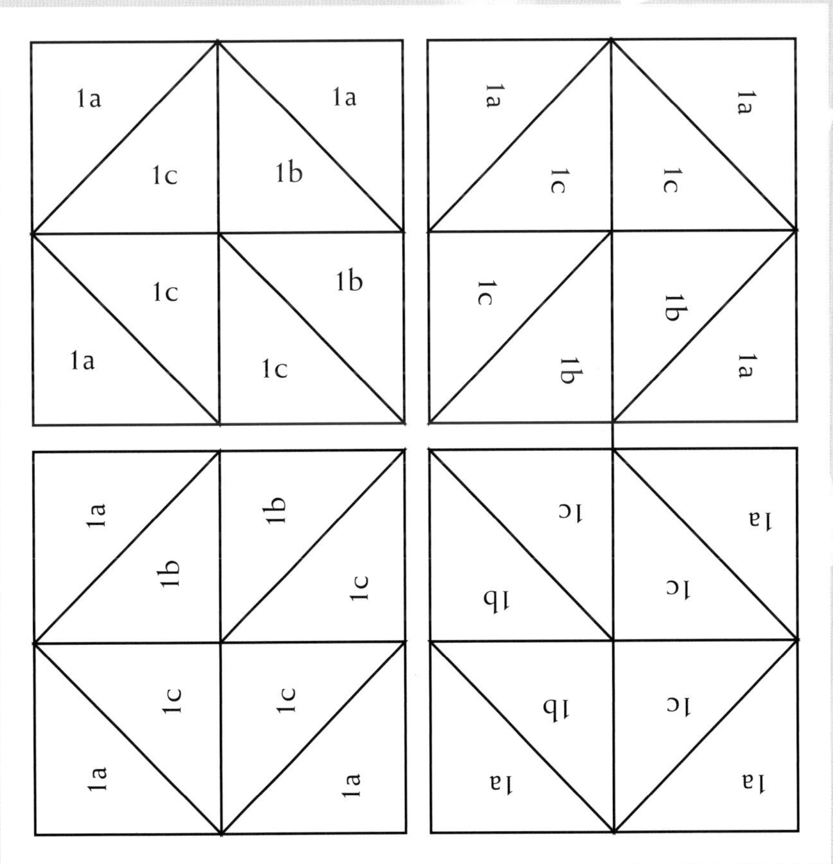
1a 1a
1c 1b
1c 1b
1a 1c
1a 1a
1c 1c
1c 1b
1b 1a
1a 1b
1b 1c
1c 1c
1a 1a
1c 1a
1b 1c
1b 1c
1a 1a

Nine-Patch Star Blocks

Tippecanoe Bed Quilt

Tippecanoe Wall Hanging

Tippecanoe Bed Quilt

Size: 91" x 106" Block #: 44 Tippecanoe
Block Size: 15" x 15" finished Number of Blocks: 20

MATERIALS
5½ yards floral print (includes third border and binding)
2 yards peach (includes second border)
1 yard gold
1½ yards light blue
2 yards medium blue (includes first border)
7½ yards backing
batting

CUTTING
8 strips, 3"-wide, medium blue (first border)
8 strips, 5½"-wide, peach (second border)
10 strips, 8½"-wide, floral print (third border)
11 strips, 2½"-wide, floral print (binding)

Tippecanoe Wall Hanging

Size: 28" x 28" Block #: 44 Tippecanoe
Block Size: 6" x 6" finished Number of Blocks: 9

MATERIALS
½ yard coral
½ yard green (includes binding)
¾ yard floral print (includes second border)
⅜ yard gold (includes first border)
1 yard backing
batting

CUTTING
4 strips, 2½"-wide, gold (first border)
4 strips, 3½"-wide, floral print (second border)
4 strips, 2½"-wide, green (binding)

Tippecanoe Mini Quilt

Size: 12" x 12" Block #: 44 Tippecanoe
Block Size: 3" x 3" finished Number of Blocks: 4

MATERIALS
fat quarter light blue (includes first border)
fat quarter dark blue (includes second border and binding)
fat quarter black
fat quarter backing
batting

CUTTING
4 strips, 1½"-wide, light blue (first border)
4 strips, 2½"-wide, dark blue (second border)
4 strips, 2½"-wide, dark blue (binding)

Tippecanoe Mini Quilt

41 Braced Star

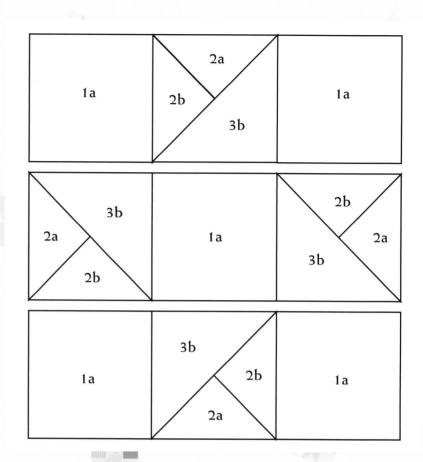

42 Mosaic Star

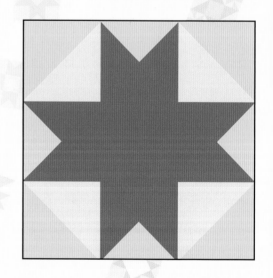

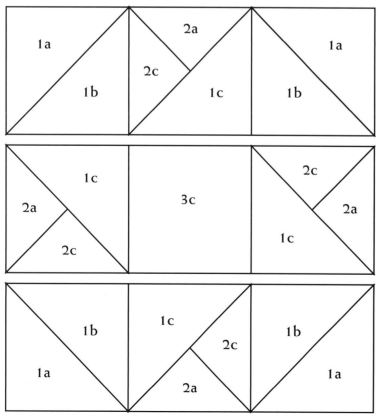

30

43 Silent Star

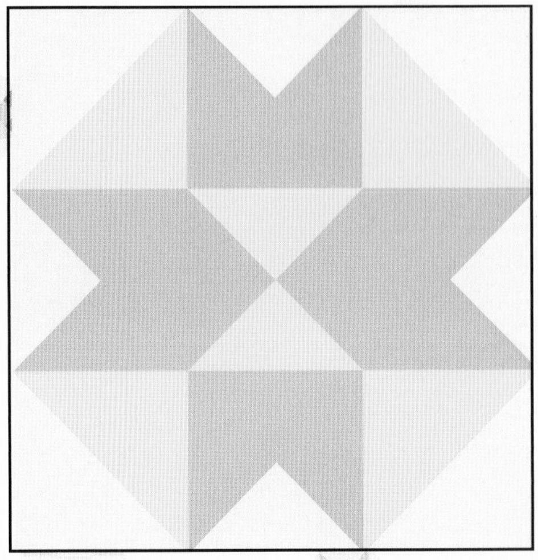

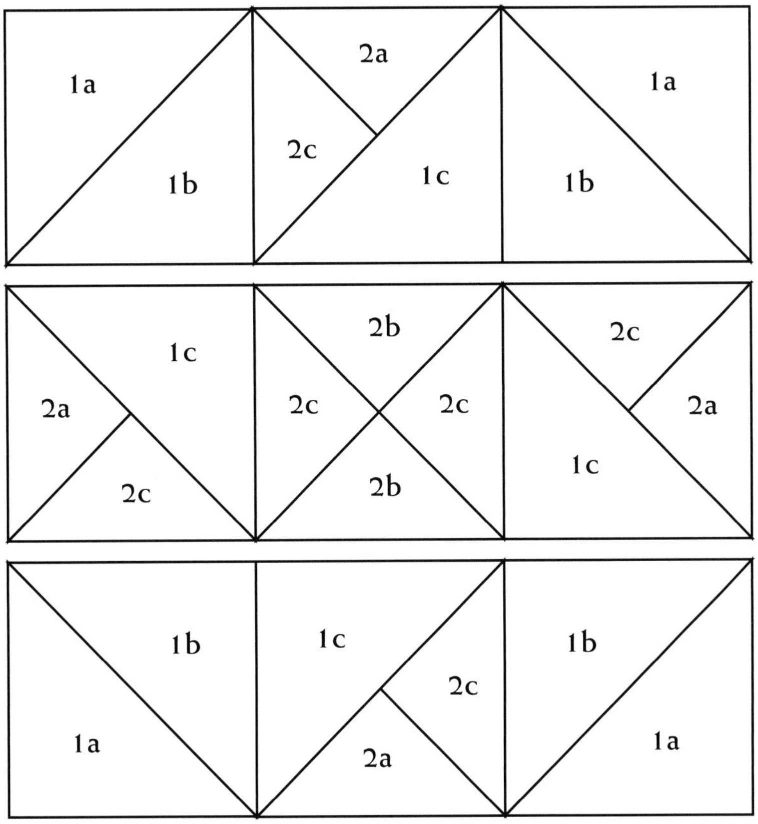
1a
1b
2a
2c
1c
1a
1b
1c
2a
2c
2b
2c
2c
2b
2c
2a
1c
1b
1a
1c
2c
2a
1b
1a

44 Tippecanoe

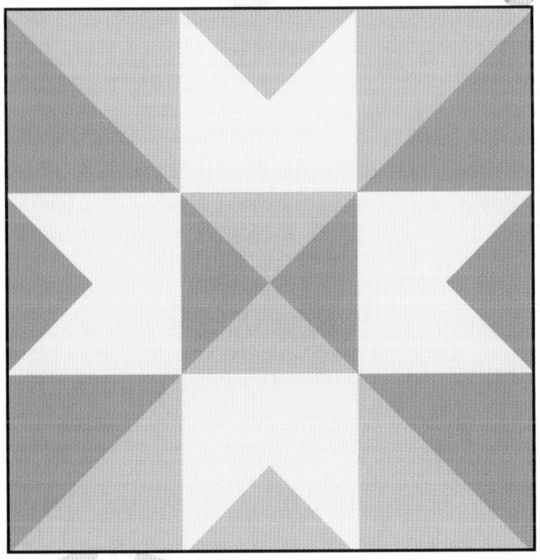

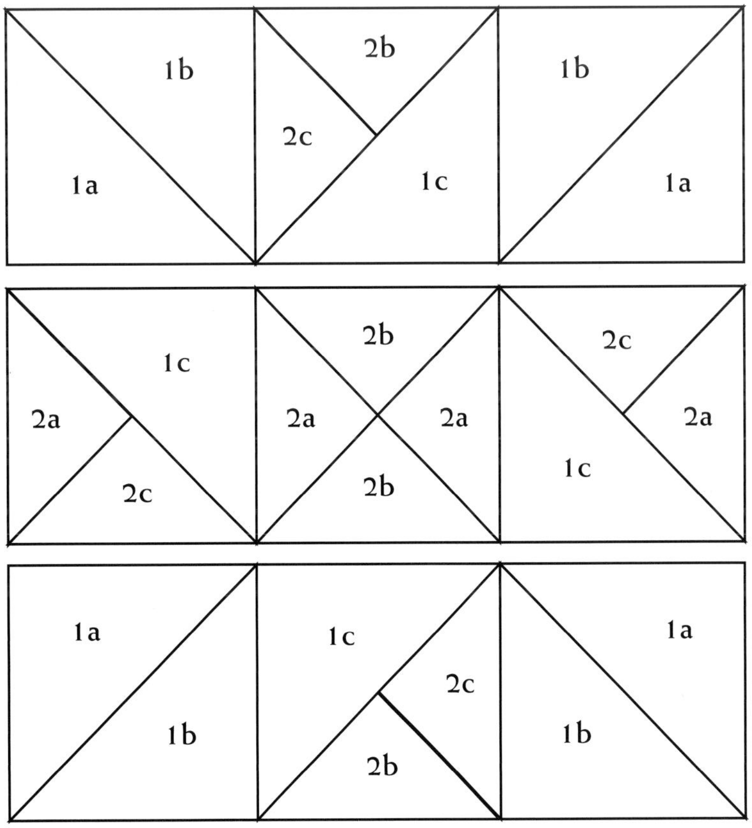
1b
1a
2b
2c
1c
1b
1a
1c
2a
2c
2b
2a
2a
2b
2c
2a
1c
1a
1b
1c
2c
2b
1a
1b

45 Variable Star

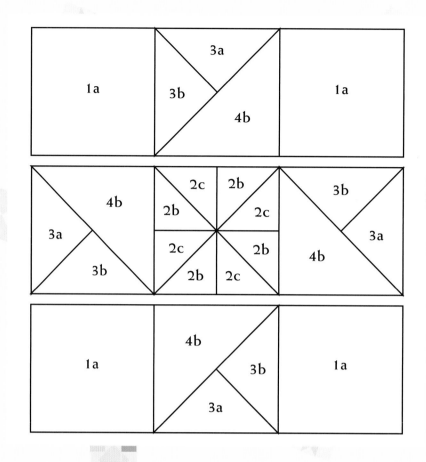

46 Western Star

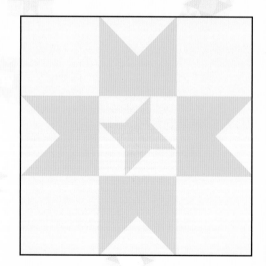

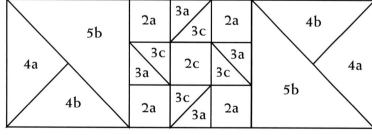

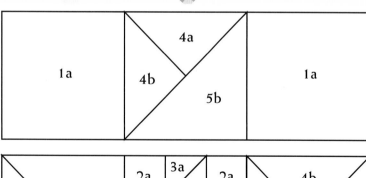

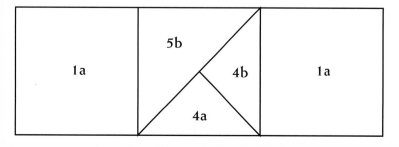

Row 1 block:

1a	1b	1a	2b	1a	1b	1a
1b	1a	1b	2c	1b	1a	1b
1a	1b	1a	3c	1a	1b	1a

Row 2 block:

| 2b / 3c / 2c | 1a 1b 1a / 1b 1a 1b / 1a 1b 1a | 2c / 3c / 2b |

Row 3 block:

1a	1b	1a	3c	1a	1b	1a
1b	1a	1b	2c	1b	1a	1b
1a	1b	1a	2b	1a	1b	1a

48 Contrary Wife

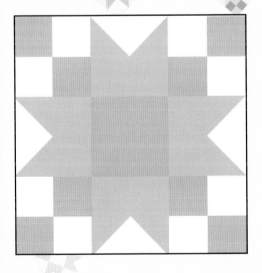

Row 1 block:

| 1a | 1b | 3b | 1b | 1a |
| 1b | 1a | 3c   4c | 1a | 1b |

Row 2 block:

| 3b / 4c / 3c | 2a | 3c / 3b / 4c |

Row 3 block:

| 1b | 1a | 4c | 1a | 1b |
| 1a | 1b | 3c / 3b | 1b | 1a |

49 Sun Rays

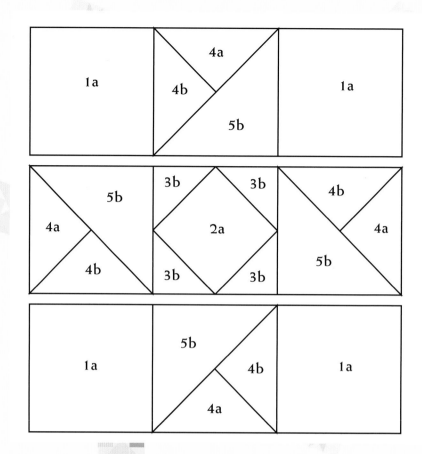

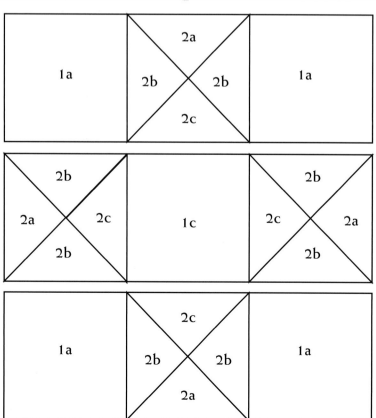

50 Nine-Patch Star

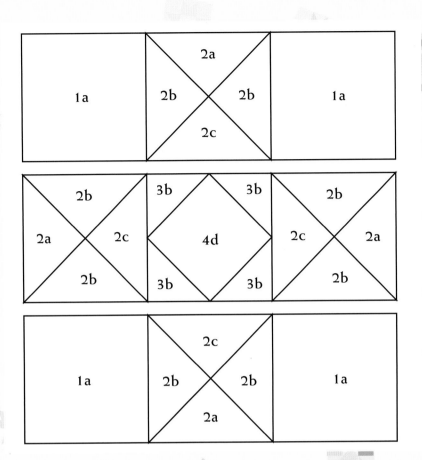

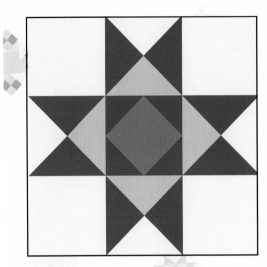

52 Ribbon Star

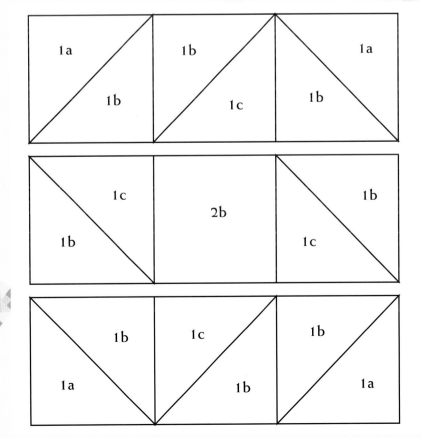

53 Whirling Star

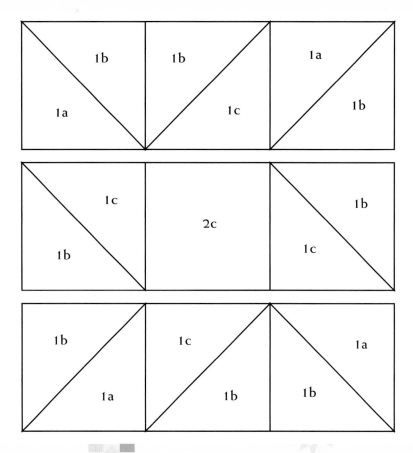

1b   1b   1a

1a   1c   1b

1c   1b

1b   2c   1c

1b   1c   1a

1a   1b   1b

54 Wandering Star

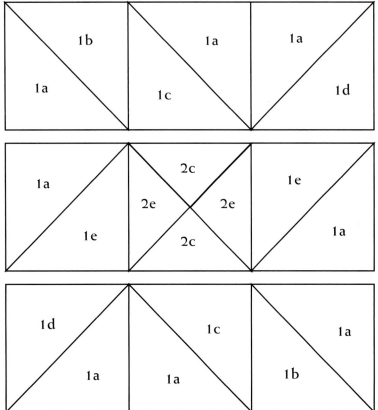

1b   1a   1a

1a   1c   1d

1a   2c   1e

1e   2e   2e   1a

     2c

1d   1c   1a

1a   1a   1b

55 Lost Star

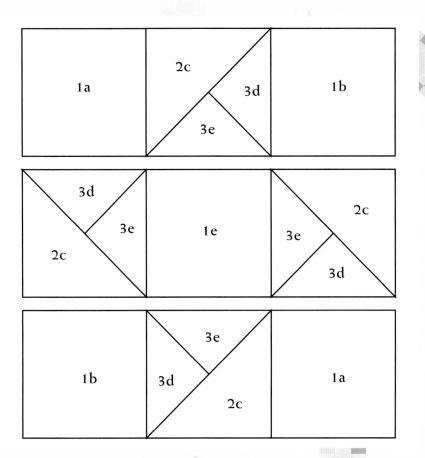

1a	2c / 3d / 3e	1b
3d / 3e / 2c	1e	3e / 2c / 3d
1b	3e / 3d / 2c	1a

56 Eccentric Star

| 1a | 1b | 4c / 3d / 3a | 1b | 1a |
| 1b | 1a | | 1a | 1b |

| 4c / 3a / 3d | 2a | 3d / 3a / 4c |

| 1b | 1a | 3a / 3d / 4c | 1a | 1b |
| 1a | 1b | | 1b | 1a |

57 Unknown Star

	3a	
1a	3b ✕ 3b	1a
	3c	

	3b	4c 5b 4c		3b	
3a ✕ 3c	5b 2c 5b	3c ✕ 3a
	3b	4c 5b 4c		3b	

	3c	
1a	3b ✕ 3b	1a
	3a	

58 Shooting Star

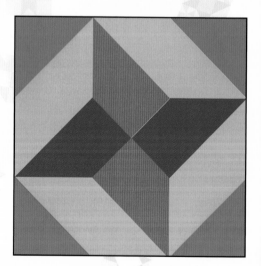

1a	1b	1a
1b	1c	1b

1b	2c	1d
1d	2d 2d	1b
	2c	

	1b	
1a	1c	1b
	1b	1a

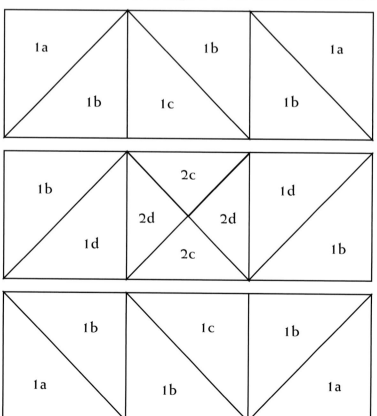

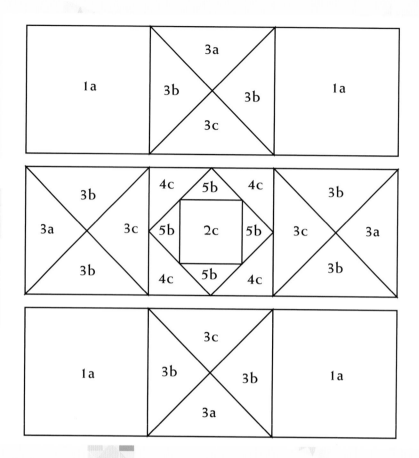

38

59 Four Corners Star

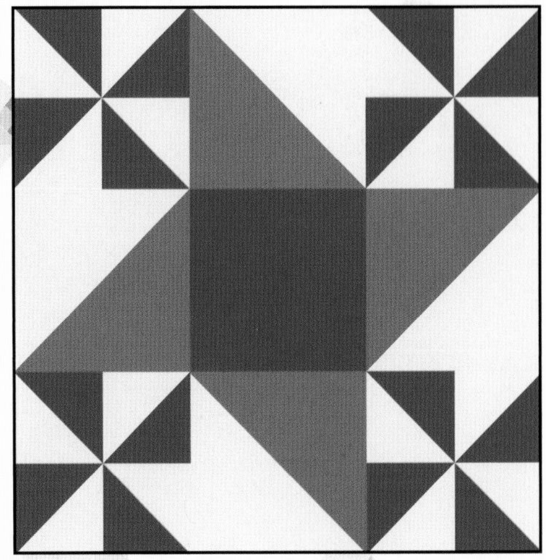

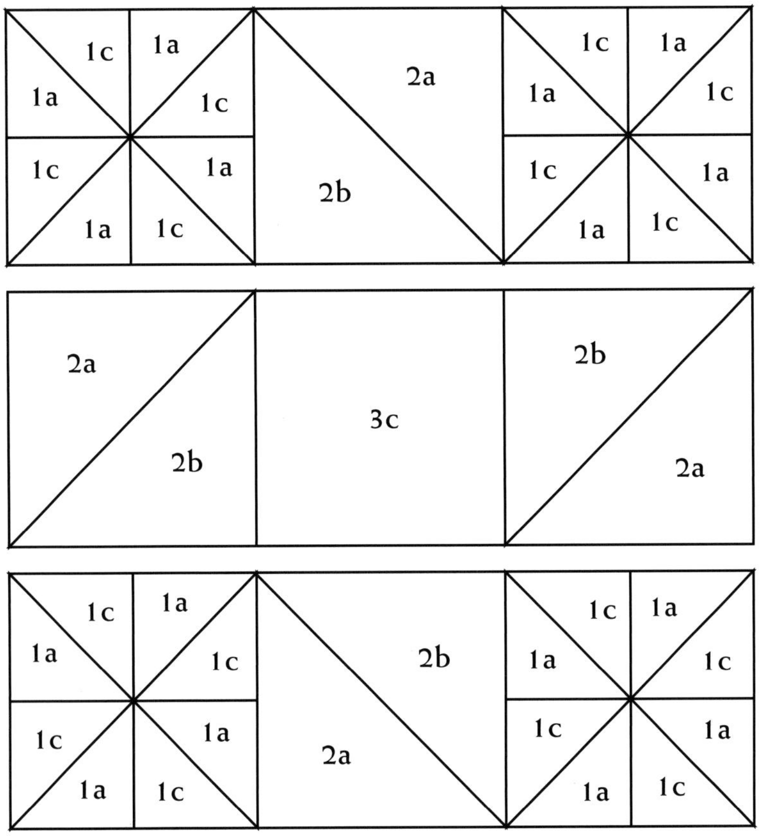
1c 1a 1a 1c 1c 1a 1a 1c
2a 2b
1c 1a 1a 1c 1c 1a 1a 1c
2a 2b
3c
2b 2a
1c 1a 1a 1c 1c 1a 1a 1c
2b 2a
1c 1a 1a 1c 1c 1a 1a 1c

60 Combination Star

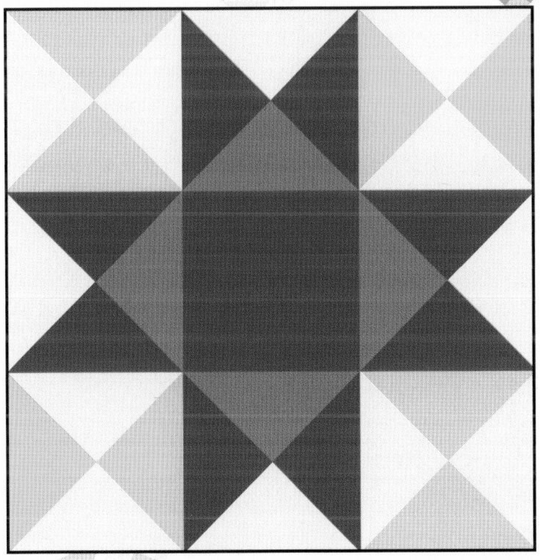

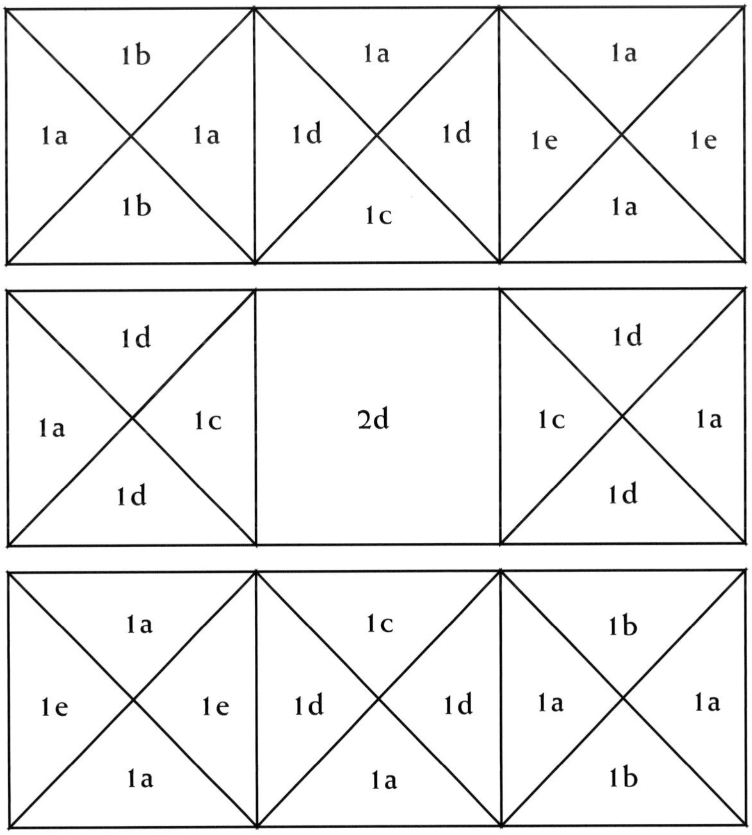
1b 1a 1a 1b
1a 1d 1d 1c
1a 1e 1e 1a
1d 1a 1c 1d
2d
1d 1c 1a 1d
1a 1e 1e 1a
1c 1d 1d 1a
1b 1a 1a 1b

Foundation Star Blocks

Royal Diamonds Bed Quilt

Royal Diamonds Wall Hanging

Royal Diamonds Mini Quilt

Royal Diamonds Bed Quilt

Size: 94" x 109" Block #: 63 Royal Diamonds
Block Size: 15" x 15" finished Number of Blocks: 20

MATERIALS
  1 yard light blue (includes first border)
  1 yard medium blue (includes third border and binding)
  1 yard light yellow
  1 yard medium yellow (includes second border)*
  1 yard light peach
  1 yard medium peach (includes second border)*
  1 yard light green
  1 yard medium green (includes second border)*
  1 yard light pink
  1 yard medium pink (includes second border)*
  9 yards backing
  batting
  * Cut strips, sew together and treat as a single border.

CUTTING
  8 strips, 3$\frac{1}{2}$"-wide, light blue (first border)
  8 strips each, 2"-wide, med pink, med peach, med yellow, med green (second border)
  11 strips, 8$\frac{1}{2}$"-wide, med blue (third border)
  11 strips, 2$\frac{1}{2}$"-wide, med blue (binding)

Royal Diamonds Wall Hanging

Size: 30" x 30" Block #: 63 Royal Diamonds
Block Size: 6" x 6" finished Number of Blocks: 9

MATERIALS
  $\frac{1}{2}$ yard white
  $\frac{1}{2}$ yard red (includes second border)
  $\frac{1}{2}$ yard light gray (includes first border)
  $\frac{1}{4}$ yard medium gray
  $\frac{3}{4}$ yard black (includes third border and binding)
  1 yard backing
  batting

CUTTING
  2 strips, 1$\frac{1}{2}$"-wide, light gray (first border)
  2 strips, 2$\frac{1}{2}$"-wide, red (second border)
  3 strips, 3$\frac{1}{2}$"-wide, black (third border)
  3 strips, 2$\frac{1}{2}$"-wide, black (binding)

Royal Diamonds Mini Quilt

Size: 13" x 13" Block #: 63 Royal Diamonds
Block Size: 3" x 3" finished Number of Blocks: 4

MATERIALS
  one fat quarter each of yellow a. yellow b, pink a, pink b, aqua (includes third border and binding), lavender (includes first border), and white (includes second border)
  fat quarter backing
  batting

CUTTING
  4 strips, 1$\frac{1}{2}$"-wide, lavender (first border)
  4 strips, 1"-wide, white (second border)
  4 strips, 2$\frac{1}{2}$"-wide, aqua (third border)
  4 strips, 2$\frac{1}{2}$"-wide, aqua (binding)

61 Lemon Star

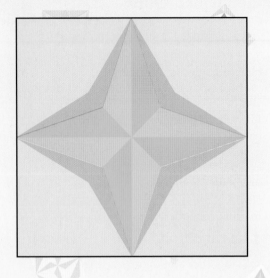

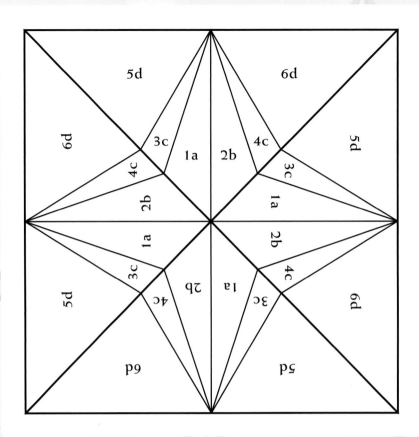

62 Star of the East

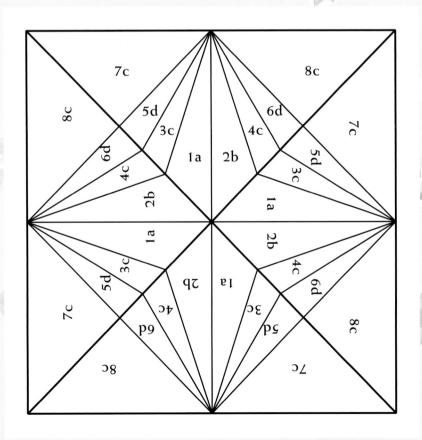

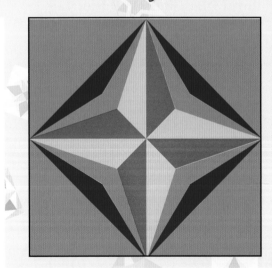

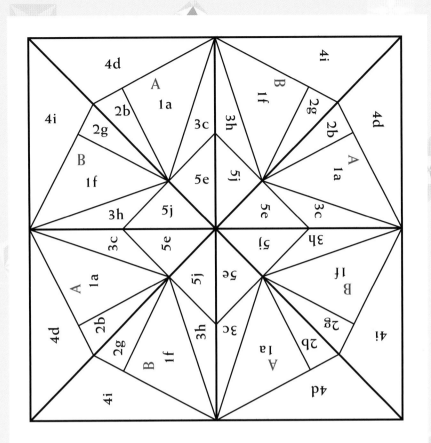

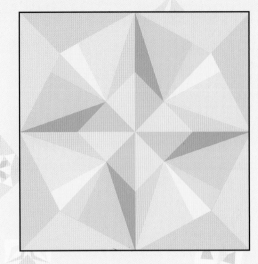

64 Morning Star

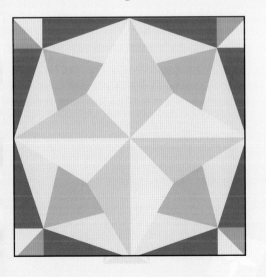

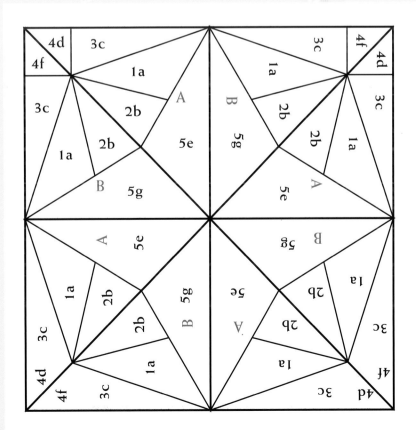

65 LeMoyne Star

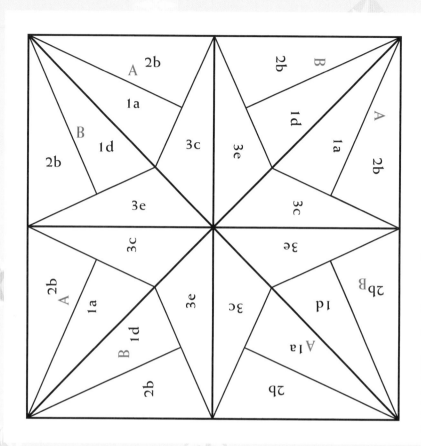

66 Bursting Star

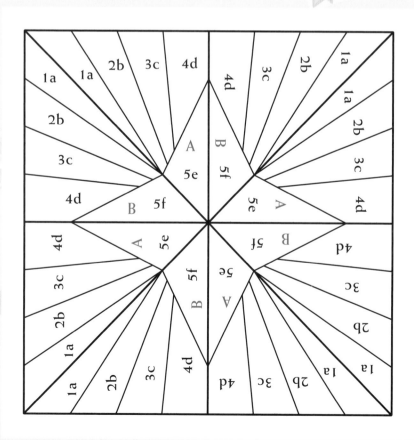

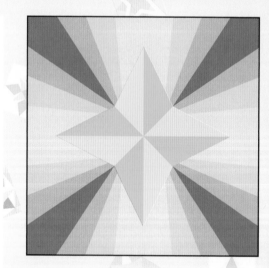

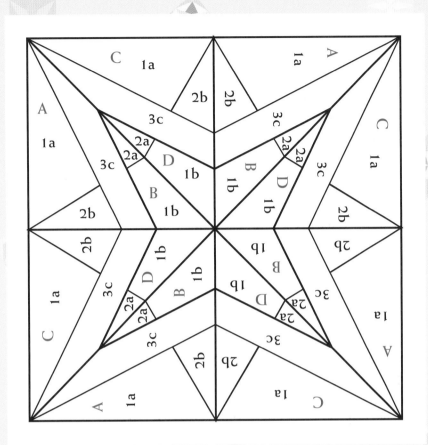

68 *Starburst*

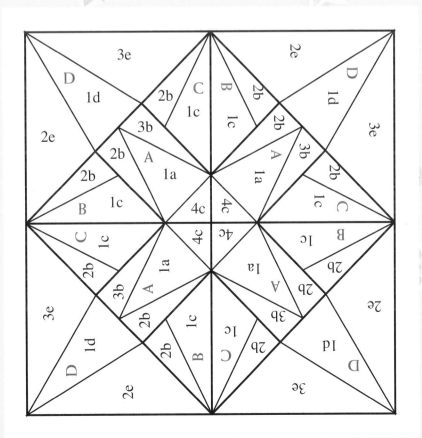

69 Star Bright

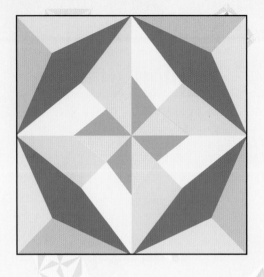

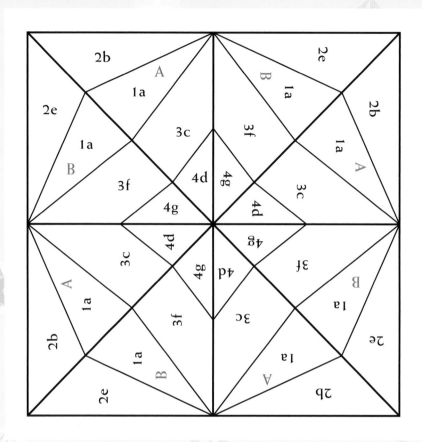

70 Star Shower

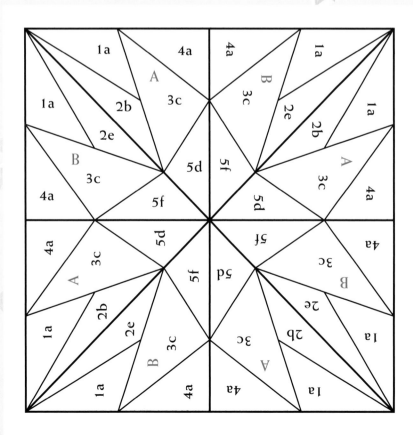

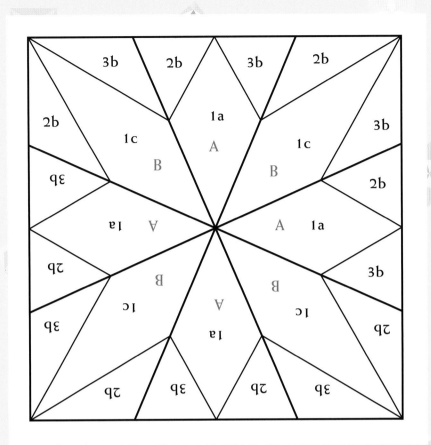

72 Star Upon a Star

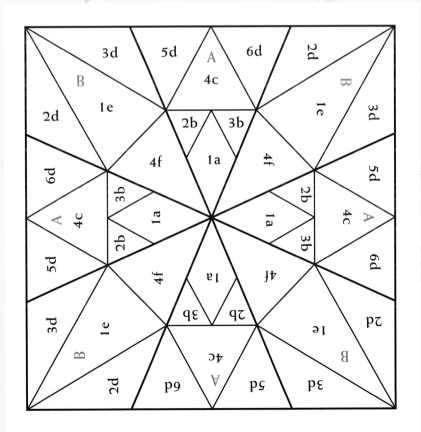

73 Triple Stars

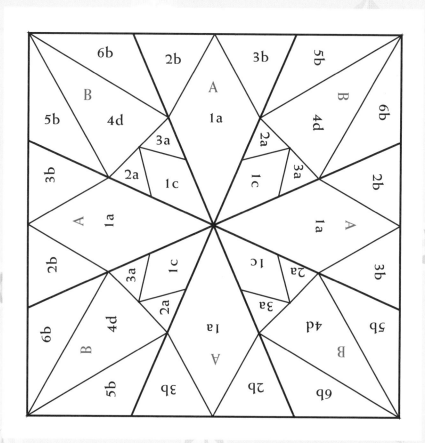

74 Diamond Head

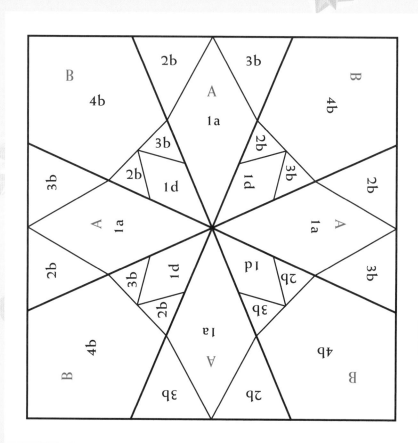

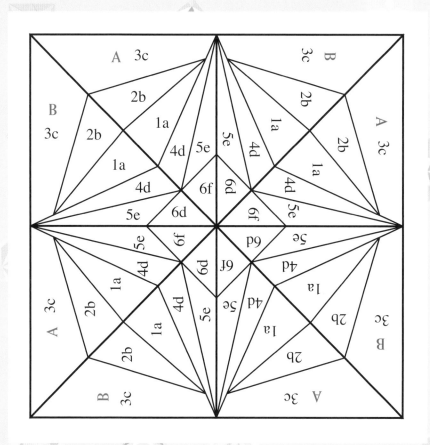

76 *Spring Bloom*

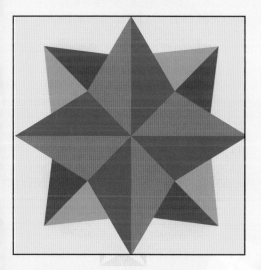

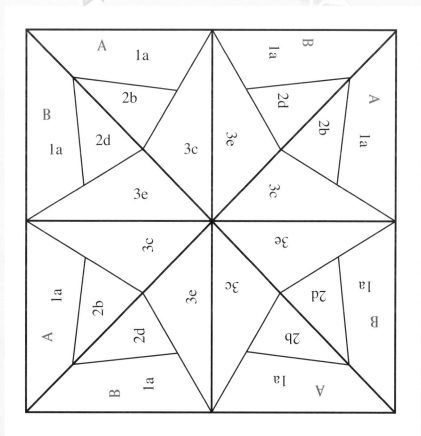

77 Simple Star

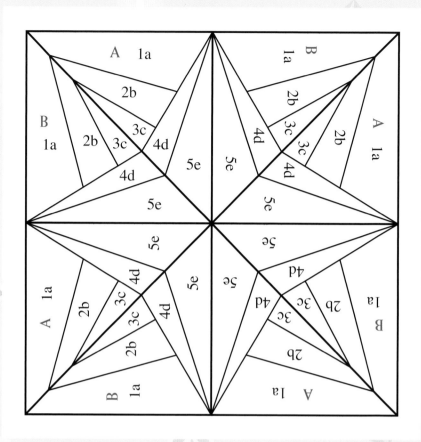

78 Crystal Star

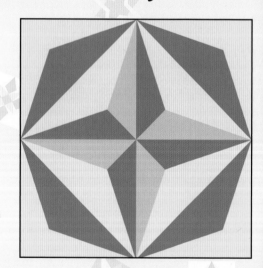

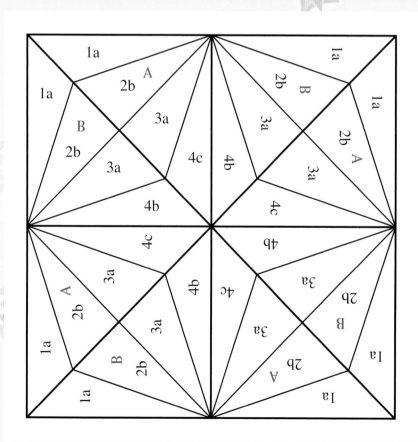

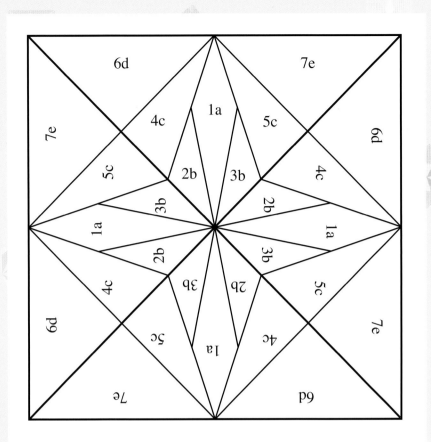

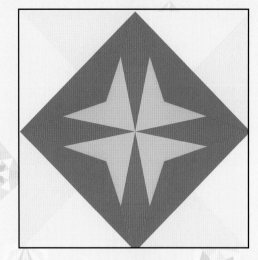

80 Octagon Star

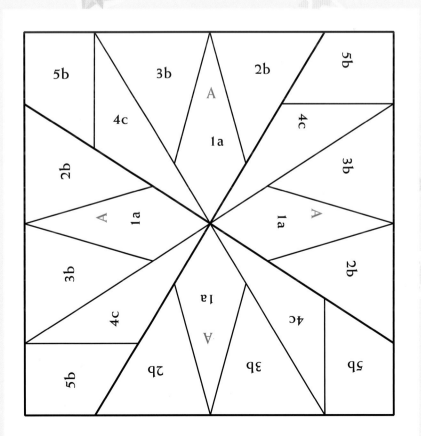

Stars and Stripes Blocks

Patriotic Stars Bed Quilt

Patriotic Stars Wall Hanging

Patriotic Stars Bed Quilt

Size: 80" x 108" Block #: 81 Patriotic Star
Block Size: 14" x 14" finished Number of Blocks: 24

MATERIALS
3 yards beige (includes second border)
3 yards brown (includes third border and binding)
2 yards black (includes first border)
1¹/₂ yards blue
1 yard burgundy
9 yards backing
batting

CUTTING
8 strips, 2¹/₂"-wide, black (first border)
9 strips, 4¹/₂"-wide, beige (second border)
10 strips, 6¹/₂"-wide, brown (third border)
11 strips, 2¹/₂"-wide, brown (binding)

Patriotic Stars Wall Hanging

Size: 36" x 36" Block #: 81 Patriotic Star
Block Size: 8" x 8" finished Number of Blocks: 9

MATERIALS
1 yard white (includes second border)
1 yard medium blue (includes first border)
1 yard dark blue (includes third border and binding)
1¹/₈ yards backing
batting

CUTTING
4 strips, 2¹/₂"-wide, medium blue (first border)
4 strips, 1¹/₂"-wide, white (second border)
4 strips, 3¹/₂"-wide, dark blue (third border)
4 strips, 2¹/₂"-wide, dark blue (binding)

Patriotic Stars Mini Quilt

Size: 12" x 12" Block #: 81 Patriotic Star
Block Size: 3" x 3" finished Number of Blocks: 4

MATERIALS
fat quarter red (includes second border)
fat quarter gold (includes binding)
fat quarter fabric blue (includes first border)
fat quarter backing
batting

CUTTING
2 strips, 1¹/₂"-wide, blue (first border)
2 strips, 2¹/₂"-wide, red (second border)
4 strips, 2¹/₂"-wide, gold (binding)

Patriotic Stars Mini Quilt

81 Patriotic Star

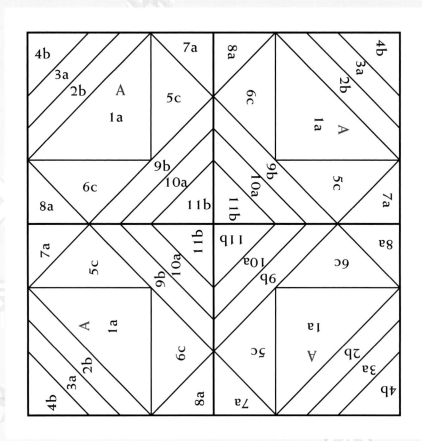

82 National Star

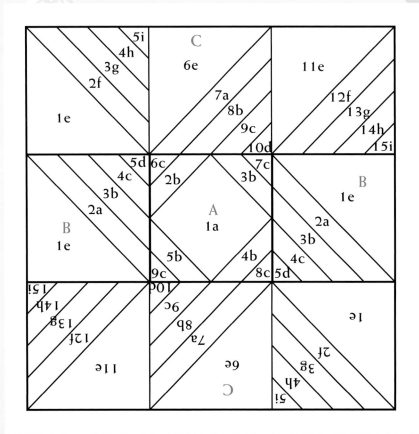

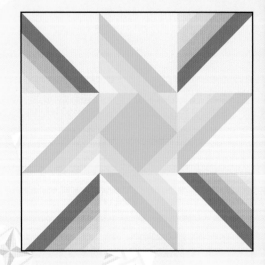

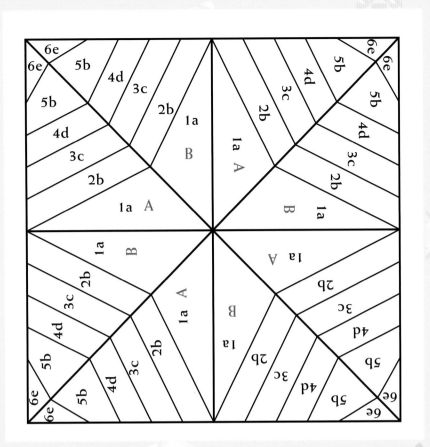

84 *Star and Stripes*

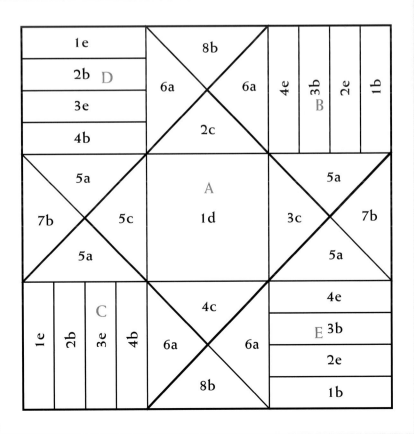

85 Liberty Star

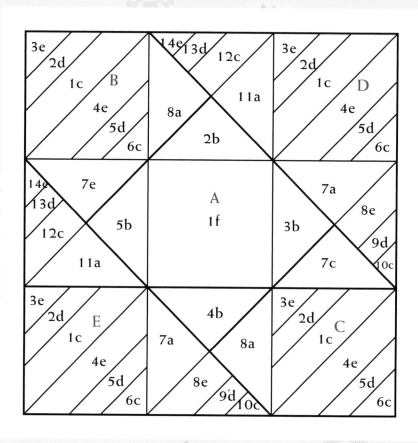

3e
2d
1c B
4e
5d
6c

14e 13d 12c
8a 11a
2b

3e
2d
1c D
4e
5d
6c

14e 7e
13d
12c
11a
5b

A
1f

7a
8e
3b
9d
7c
10c

3e
2d E
1c
4e
5d
6c

4b
7a 8a
8e
9d 10c

3e
2d C
1c
4e
5d
6c

86 All-American Star

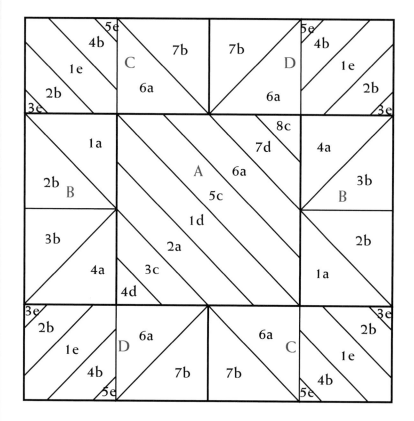

5e
4b
1e C 7b 7b D
2b 6a 6a
3e

5e
4b
1e
2b
3e

1a
2b B
3b
4a

8c
7d
A 6a 4a
5c 3b B
1d 2b
2a
3c 1a
4d

3e
2b
1e D 6a
4b 7b 7b
5e

6a
C
1e
2b
4b
5e

56

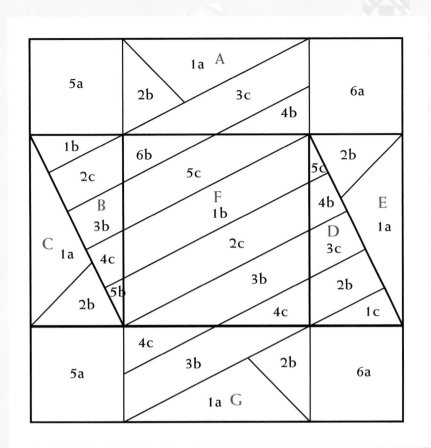

5a

1a A
2b 3c
4b

6a

1b
2c
6b
5c
2b
5c

B
3b
F
1b
4b
E
1a

C
1a
4c
2c
D
3c

5b
3b

2b
4c
2b

1c

4c
3b
2b

5a
1a G
6a

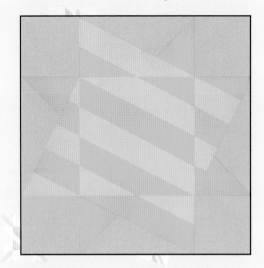

88 Patriot's Star

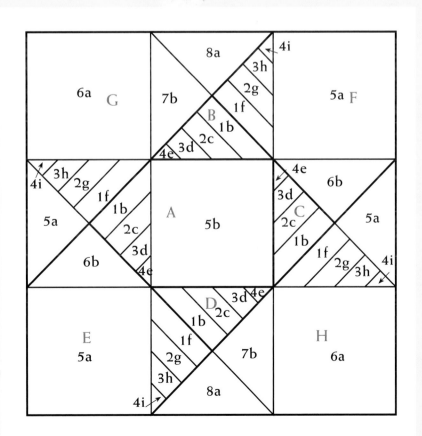

6a G
7b
8a
4i
3h
2g
1f
5a F

B
1b
2c
3d
4e

4i
3h
2g
1f
1b
2c
3d
4e
5a
A
5b
6b
4e
3d
C
2c
1b
1f
2g 3h
4i
6b
5a

E
5a
D
2c 3d 4e
1b
1f
2g
3h
4i
7b
8a
H
6a

89 Stars and Stripes Forever

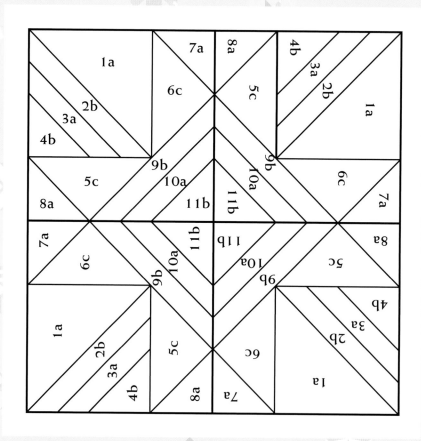

90 Star Spangled

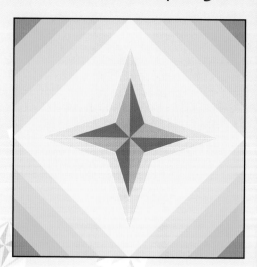

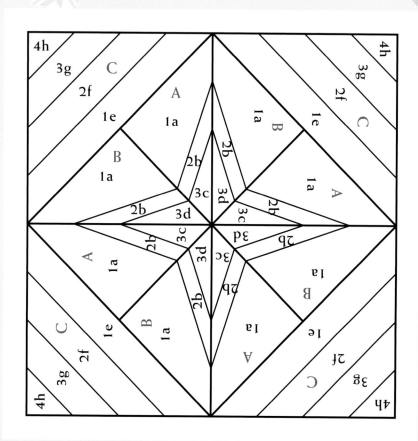

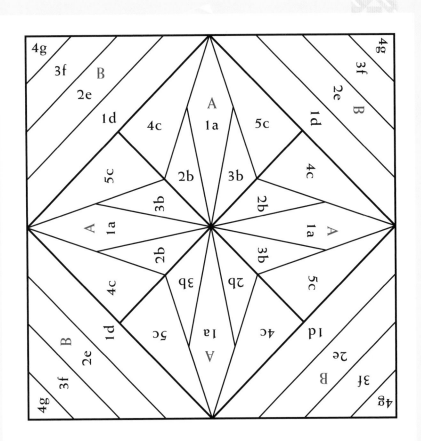

Within the diagram for 91 Star of Many Colors:

4g 3f B 2e 1d 4c 1a A 5c 1d 2e B 3f 4g
5c 2b 3b 4c
A 1a 3b 2b 1a A
4c 3b 2b 5c
1d 5c 1a A 4c 1d
B 2e 3f 2e B
4g 3f 4g

92 *America's Pride*

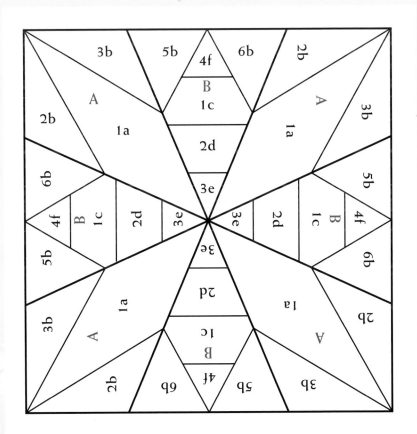

Within the diagram for 92 America's Pride:

3b 5b 4f 6b 2b
B 1c
A 2d A
2b 3b
3e
6b 5b
4f B 1c 2d 3e 3e 2d B 1c 4f 6b
5b 3e
1a 2d 1a
A B 1c A
3b 5b 4f 6b 3b
2b 6b 4f 5b 3b
2b

59

93 President's Star

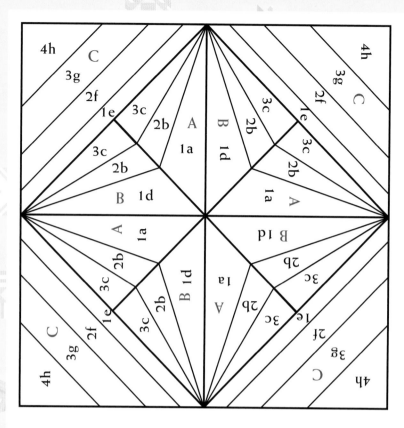

94 Shining Star

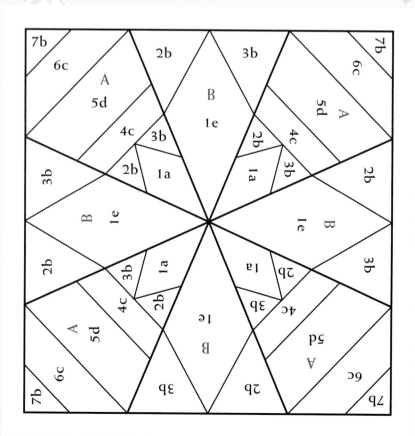

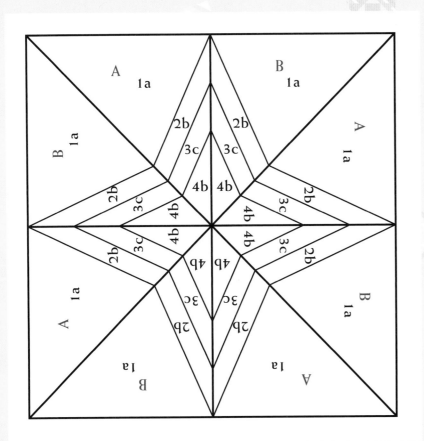

96 Red, White and Blue

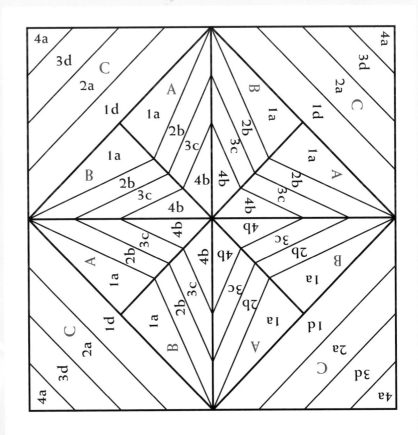

97 My Country

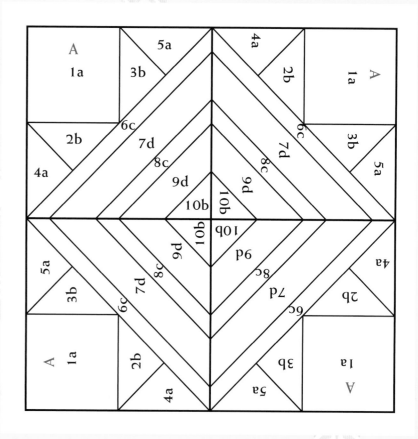

98 Stripes in a Star

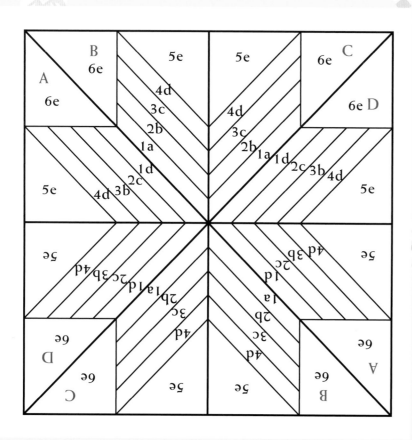

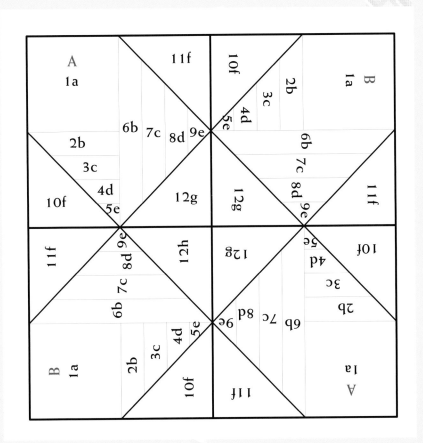

100 *Patriotic Block*

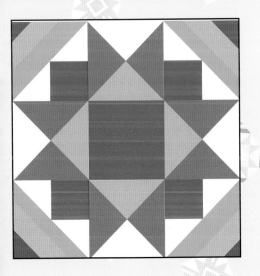

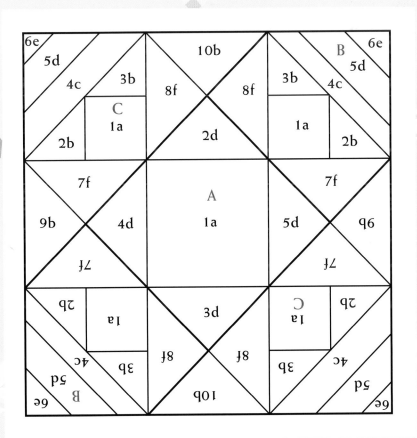

General Directions

There are two different types of blocks in this book: blocks that use templates and blocks that use foundation piecing. The diagrams given with each block indicate what type of block. For example, diagrams shown as complete blocks, are foundation pieced. **(Diagram 1)**

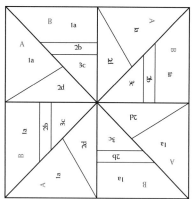

Diagram 1

Blocks that use templates are shown as nine patches or four patches.**(Diagram 2)**

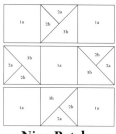

Nine Patch
Diagram 2

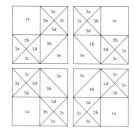

Four Patch

Spinning Stars and Whirligigs (pages 6 to 15), Foundation Stars (pages 42 to 51) and Stars and Stripes Blocks (pages 54 to 63) all use foundation patterns. Four-Patch Stars (pages 18-27) and Nine-Patch Stars(pages 30-39) use templates.

If you'd like to use templates instead of foundation patterns, just make templates referring to Sewing with Templates, page 67.

FOUNDATION PIECING

Materials

Before you begin, decide the kind of foundation on which you are planning to piece the blocks.

Since the blocks in this book are printed from a CD using your computer and printer, the most popular choice for a foundation is regular copy paper since it is readily available. You can also use freezer paper. It comes in sheets by C. Jenkins or a roll by Reynolds®. If you use the roll, you will have to cut sheets that will fit through your printer. If using freezer paper, be sure to

print the pattern on the dull side. Then as you piece, use a small craft iron or a travel iron to press fabric pieces in place on the foundation after sewing each seam. The paper is removed once the blocks are completely sewn.

There are other options for foundation materials that can be used with your computer and printer. One type is Tear Away™ or Fun-dation™, translucent non-woven materials, combining the advantages of both paper and fabric. They are easy to see through, and like paper, they can be removed with ease. Another foundation material is one that dissolves in water after use called Dissolve Away Foundation Paper by EZ Quilting®.

Preparing the Foundation

Since the Block Patterns are given in several sizes on a CD, preparing your foundation is easier than ever. All you need to do is decide which block you would like to make (from 2" to 8" square) and which size you will need for your quilt. Place the CD in your computer, choose the block and print the number of copies that you will need for your quilt.

The blocks on the CD range in size from 2" to 8" square since those are the sizes that will fit on a regular sheet of paper. For those that are larger than an 8½" x 11" sheet of paper, you may need to go to your local copier store to print the blocks on 11" x 17" paper. See Frequently Asked Questions on the CD for guidelines on printing blocks over 8" square.

Cutting the Fabric

In foundation piecing, you do not have to cut perfect shapes! You can, therefore, use odd pieces of fabric: squares, strips, and rectangles. The one thing you must remember, however, is that every piece must be at least ¼" larger on all sides than the space it is going to cover. Strips and squares are easy: just measure the length and width of the needed space and add ½" all around. Cut your strip to that measurement. Triangles, however, can be a bit tricky. In that case, measure the widest point of the triangle and cut your fabric about ½" to 1" wider.

Other Supplies for Foundation Piecing

You will need a cleaned and oiled sewing machine, glue stick, pins, paper scissors, fabric scissors, and foundation material.

Before beginning to sew your actual block by machine, determine the proper stitch length. Use a piece of the paper you are planning to use for the foundation and draw a straight line on it. Set your machine so that it sews with a fairly short stitch (about 20 stitches per inch). Sew along the line. If you can tear the paper apart with ease, you are sewing with the right length. You don't want to sew with such a short stitch that the paper falls apart by itself.

Using a Pattern

The numbers on the block show the order in which the pieces are to be placed and sewn on the foundation. It is extremely important that you follow the numbers; otherwise the entire process won't work. The letters refer to the fabrics used in the finished block shown. When choosing fabric, assign a letter to each fabric. Sew the asigned fabric to the corresponding space on the pattern.

Making the Block

The important thing to remember about making a foundation block is that the fabric goes on the unmarked side of the foundation while you sew on the printed side. The finished block is a mirror image of the original pattern.

Step 1: Hold the foundation up to a light source—even a window—with the unmarked side facing you. Find the space marked 1 on the unmarked side and put a dab of glue there. Place the fabric right side up on the overlaps at least ¹/₄" on all sides of space 1. **(Diagram 3)**

Step 2: Fold the foundation along the line between Space 1 and Space 2. Cut the fabric so that it is ¹/₄" from the fold. **(Diagram 4)**

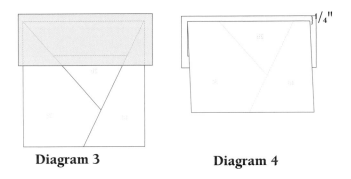

Diagram 3   **Diagram 4**

Step 3: With right sides together, place Fabric Piece 2 on Fabric Piece 1, making sure that the edge of Piece 2 is even with the just-trimmed edge of Piece 1. **(Diagram 5)**

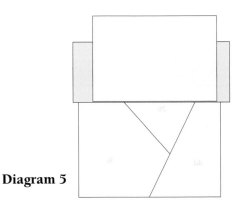

Diagram 5

Step 4: To make certain that Piece 2 will cover Space 2, fold the fabric piece back along the line between Space 1 and Space 2. **(Diagram 6)**

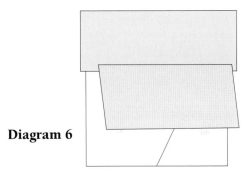

Diagram 6

Step 5: With the marked side of the foundation facing up, place the piece on the sewing machine (or sew by hand), holding both Piece 1 and Piece 2 in place. Sew along the line between Space 1 and Space 2. **(Diagram 7)**

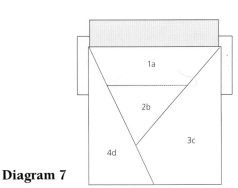

Diagram 7

Hint: *If you use a small stitch, it will be easier to remove the paper later. Start stitching about two or three stitches before the beginning of the line and end your sewing two or three stitches beyond the line, allowing the stitches to be held in place by the next round of stitching rather than by backstitching.*

Step 6: Turn the work over and open Piece 2. Press the seam open. **(Diagram 8)**

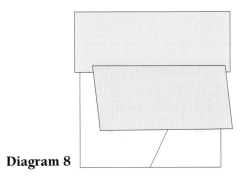

Diagram 8

Step 7: Turning the work so that the marked side is on top, fold the foundation forward along the line between Space 1+2 and Space 3. Trim about 1/8" to 1/4" from the fold. It is easier to trim the fabric if you pull the paper away from the stitching. If you use fabric as your foundation, fold the fabric forward as far as it will go and then start to trim. **(Diagram 9)**

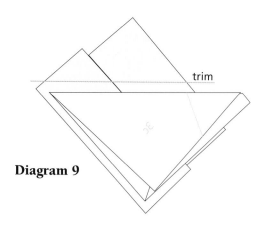

Diagram 9

Step 8: Place Fabric Piece 3 right side down even with the just-trimmed edge. **(Diagram 10)**

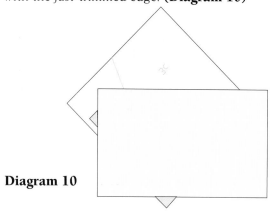

Diagram 10

Step 9: Turn the block over to the marked side and sew along the line between Space 1+2 and Space 3. **(Diagram 11)**

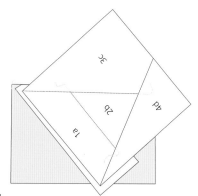

Diagram 11

Step 10: Turn the work over, open Piece 3 and press open. **(Diagram 12)**

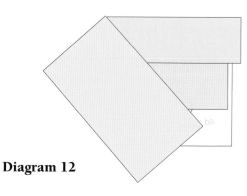

Diagram 12

Step 11: In the same way you have added the other pieces, add Piece #4 to complete this block. Trim the fabric 1/4" from the edge of the foundation. The foundation-pieced block is completed. **(Diagram 13)**

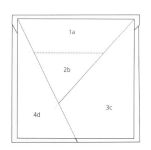 

Diagram 13

Note: *The finished block is a mirror image to the pattern used to complete the sewing.*

After you have finished sewing a block, don't immediately remove the paper. Since you are often piecing with tiny bits of fabric, grainline is not a factor. Therefore, some of the pieces may have been cut on the bias and may have a tendency to stretch. You can eliminate any problem with distortion by keeping the paper in place until all of the blocks have been sewn together. If, however, you want to remove the paper, stay stitch along the outer edge of the block to help keep the block in shape.

Sewing Multiple Sections

Many of the blocks in foundation piecing are created with two or more sections. These sections, which are indicated by letters, are individually pieced and then sewn together. The cutting line for these sections is indicated by a bold line. Before you start to make any of these multi-section blocks, begin by cutting the foundation piece apart so that each section is worked independently. Leave a 1/4" seam allowance around each section.

Step 1: Following the previous instructions for Making the Block, complete each section. Then place the sections right sides together. Pin the corners of the top section to the corners of the bottom section. **(Diagram 14)**

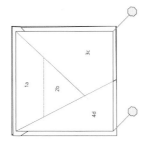

Diagram 14

Step 2: When you are certain that the pieces are aligned correctly, sew the two sections together using the regular stitch length on the sewing machine.

Step 3: Press the sections open and continue sewing the sections in pairs. **(Diagram 15)**

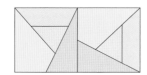

Diagram 15

Step 4: Sew necessary pairs of sections together to complete the block. **(Diagram 16)**

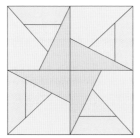

Diagram 16

What You Don't Want to Forget

1. If you plan to sew by hand, begin by taking some backstitches that will anchor the thread at the beginning of the line. Then use a backstitch every four or five stitches. End the stitching with a few backstitches.

2. If you plan to sew by machine, start stitching two or three stitches before the start of the stitching line and finish your stitching two or three stitches beyond the end.

3. Use a short stitch (about 20 stitches per inch) for paper foundations to make it easier to remove the paper. If the paper falls apart as you sew, your stitches are too short.

4. Press each seam as you finish it.

5. Stitching which goes from a space into another space will not interfere with adding additional fabric pieces.

6. Remember to trim all seam allowances at least 1/4".

7. When sewing points, start from the wide end and sew towards the point.

8. Unless you plan to use it only once in the block, it is a good idea to stay away from directional prints in foundation piecing.

9. When cutting pieces for foundation piecing, never worry about the grainline.

10. Always remember to sew on the marked side, placing the fabric on the unmarked side.

11. Follow the numerical order, or it won't work.

12. Once you have finished making a block do not remove the paper until the entire quilt has been finished unless you stay stitch around the outside of the block.

13. Be sure that the ink you use to make your foundation is permanent and will not wash out into your fabric.

Making Blocks with Templates

Templates are used to complete some of the blocks in this book. The template blocks are either nine-patch or four-patch blocks. The block diagrams are shown in the book next to the finished blocks; they are split into four-patch or nine-patch blocks. The different pattern pieces within the block are numbered. For example, in **Diagram 17**, the star block has four different pattern pieces: 1,2, 3 and 4. The letters refer to fabric choices.

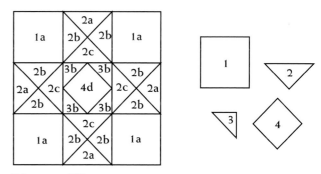

Diagram 17

Find your block on the enclosed CD and choose the size you will need to complete your project. Print out the block patterns.

1. Trace each pattern individually onto clear template plastic. Be sure to trace the patterns far apart enough to add a ¼" seam allowance. **(Diagram 18)** This will be your sewing line if you are hand piecing. Label each pattern piece.

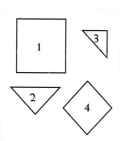

Diagram 18

2. If you are going to machine piece, add ¼" seam allowance along all sides of template. **(Diagram 19)** This will be your cutting line.

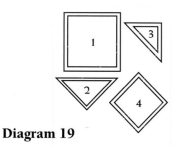

Diagram 19

3. Cut out out each pattern along cutting line. **(Diagram 20)**

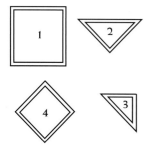

Diagram 20

4. Trace each template onto the wrong side of the fabric chosen for the individual template, tracing the number of patterns needed for your project. **(Diagram 21)**

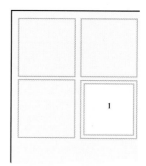

Diagram 21

5. Carefully cut out each piece.

Hint: *Keep cut pieces in a labeled recloseable plastic bag.*

6. Sew the number of blocks needed to complete your quilt.